A WOUND[...]

A WOUNDED CHURCH

Religion, Politics and Justice in Ireland

Joseph McVeigh

THE MERCIER PRESS
CORK AND DUBLIN

The Mercier Press, 4 Bridge Street, Cork
24 Lower Abbey Street, Dublin 1

British Library Cataloguing in Publication Data
McVeigh, Joseph
    A Wounded Church: Religion, Politics and Justice
    in Ireland.
    1. Ireland. Catholic Church. Relations with state.
    I. Title
    322'.1'09415

ISBN 0 85342 886 7

Printed by Litho Press Co., Midleton, Co. Cork.

Contents

Introduction

THE CHURCH AND SOCIAL JUSTICE

*'Actions on behalf of justice and participation
in the transformation of the world
fully appear to us as a constitutive dimension of
the preaching of the Gospel or in other words,
of the Church's mission for the redemption
of the human race and its liberation
from every oppressive situation.'*
(1971 WORLD SYNOD OF BISHOPS:*Justice In The World*)

The Church — the People of God, as defined by the Second
Vatican Council — has a purpose to continue the work of Christ
on earth. That work is to help realise the Kingdom of God, a
kingdom of love, truth, justice and peace in a world where,
because of structural injustice, the poor, who are the majority, are
denied their basic human rights. The Second Vatican Council
decreed that the Church, in order to carry out its mission
effectively, should 'read the signs of the times', a Biblical way of
saying that the Church must analyse its own historical role and
make an option for the poor.

The Church, though not about gaining power for itself, has a
political role in society because it is a social organisation. Within
society the Church can either be a supporter of the political and
economic status quo which favours the rich and powerful or a
challenge to it which is its unique prophetic role. Unfortunately,
the official Church has often lost sight of its original prophetic
mission to be a critic of the worldly powers.

The Catholic Church's historical role in Europe since
Constantine in the fourth century has been in support of the
political status quo even when that status quo was inherently
corrupt. The Church has traditionally favoured the monarchical
form of government and opposed the people's struggles for
independence and democracy. Not so long ago the Catholic
Church collaborated with Franco in Spain and with other fascist

regimes in Europe. Church leaders have supported unjust colonial regimes not just in Ireland but in Latin America and elsewhere. In supporting the political status quo Church leaders felt that it was in the best interests of the Church as an institution. The preservation of the institution became all important.

It is sometimes said that the Church is now at the beginning of its third historical epoch. The first period was from Christ until Constantine, the Church of the Catacombs, when the Church was persecuted because it was seen as a threat to the Empire; the second, from Constantine until the Second Vatican Council, when the hierarchical Church officially supported the status quo. The third began with the Second Vatican Council, which distanced the Church from the secular powers and pointed a new model of the Church in the direction of the powerless and oppressed.

There has been a growing awareness that in order to carry out its prophetic role, as Servant of the Poor, the Church ought to be completely free and independent of secular powers and governments — no matter how well disposed they may appear to be. Above all it is felt that no sector of the Church ought to allow itself to be used by any government or secular power even in return for certain favours or 'privileges'.

One of the main challenges facing the leaders of the Catholic Church in many countries today is how to help resolve conflicts which result from the denial of basic human rights by governments. In these conflicts the Church leaders cannot remain neutral. Given the Church's understanding of its mission as helping to build the Kingdom of God, it has no option but to side with the weak and powerless.

According to the Second Vatican Council the search for social justice concerns all of the people of God — all members of the Church, but especially bishops, priests and religious. It is intrinsic to the Christian faith. One of the editors of the Kairos document in South Africa comments:

> ... As a church we have an obligation to reread the Bible, to reinterpret our faith, to begin liberating ourselves from the ecclesiastical traditions that have been developed in the interests of those who dominate society.[1]

Social justice must be given a high priority on the Church leaders' agenda. Historically, this has not been the case:

... historically, the church has identified itself with the powerful, and has developed its theology from this perspective. The Church went along with the colonisation process, and supported many of the atrocities that were committed...[2]

The Second Vatican Council heralded a change in the Church's attitude to the problems facing the poor in the world and to their struggles for liberation. At the 1971 Synod of Bishops there was a recognition of the Church's mission as Servant to those who are oppressed in the world;

The mission of preaching the Gospel dictates at the present time that we should dedicate ourselves to the liberation of people even in their present existence in this world. For unless the Christian message of love and justice shows its effectiveness through action in the cause of justice in the world, it will only with difficulty gain credibility with the people of our times.[3]

The Catholic Church in Ireland has its own particular history which helps to explain the present silence of the Catholic bishops about the oppression of Irish nationalists forced to live under British colonial rule. That history, involving as it does close links with the Vatican, also explains their reluctance to confront the British government. One of the first difficulties in Ireland is that the Catholic Church has become very much a hierarchical Church, so much so that the word 'Church' is often used to mean the hierarchy and vice versa. This equation of the Church with the hierarchy which is completely at variance with the Second Vatican Council's description, of the Church as *The People of God*, results in a very authoritarian Church in which the bishops speak and their people obey. There is little dialogue or social interaction between the poor and the Church leaders.

Within the past twenty years, however, mainly as a result of the influence of Irish missionaries, the Catholic Church in Ireland at all levels, has taken up the cause of the poor in countries around the world (e.g. Trocaire, Afri, etc.) while some home-based priests and religious have become involved in social justice issues in the twenty-six counties. Some priests and religious led the opposition to President Reagan's visit in 1984 while the Irish Catholic bishops ignored him because of his repressive policies in Central America.

Many Church groups joined with political groups and the Trade Union Movement in campaigning against the Single European Act in 1987 in opposition to the Confederation of Irish Industry, the Irish Farmers Association and the main political parties in the south. They have consistently condemned the Dublin government policies with regard to chronic unemployment and enforced emigration but have failed to relate the failure of the twenty-six county economy to partition. There is a contradiction when Catholic Church groups, including bishops, express deep concern about the denial of human rights in some distant country and ignore that same reality at home. This contradiction of what is called 'long-distance Christianity' needs to be confronted. (Already a small number of Catholics involved with the Resource publications in Dublin have begun to question the official Catholic Church's attitude to the ongoing conflict in the north).

The British government continues to regard the Catholic bishops in Ireland as useful in carrying out its policy of undermining the Irish people's struggle for national self-determination and independence. As the British government runs out of political options it relies more than ever on the support of leaders in the Catholic Church to maintain control in Ireland.[4] This alliance must surely bring the Catholic bishops into conflict with their own people.

The introduction of more and more repressive laws in the six counties by the British government (e.g., censorship, ending the right to silence), further underlines the violent and corrupt nature of the northern statelet which can only be governed by armed force and repression; and yet the Catholic hierarchy has failed to make a moral judgement on this unjust system.

The role adopted by the Catholic hierarchy is no longer acceptable to a large section within the Church. The origins of this division and conflict within the Catholic Church in Ireland need to be examined from the viewpoint of the oppressed if that conflict is to be resolved. The first part of the book (chapters 1-3) examines the historical context. The second part of the book (chapters 4-6) examines the historical relationships of church and state and the present conflict between the theology of liberation and the pro-establishment theology of obedience. The third part of the book (chapters 7-9) deals with the urgent question now facing all Catholics in Ireland — what kind of Church do we Catholics want in Ireland — a Church of the Rich and Powerful which supports the political status quo by refusing to confront the British government's continued interference in Irish affairs — or a Church of the Poor and Oppressed which condemns British injustice in Ireland? Do we want a reformed, modernised Church that is content to pursue 'lay involvement', 'reconciliation' and even political reform but which does not confront British injustice, the root cause of division and conflict? Or, do we want a radically different Church which by its concern for the oppressed and willingness to talk to elected representatives including Sinn Féin, witnesses to the Truth? Do we want a Church in which the hierarchy and clergy are involved with the British government in social control, or do we want a Church where bishops, priests and religious join with the oppressed Irish nationalists of the north in their struggle for social justice and call on the clergy and leaders of the other Churches to join with them in this struggle? Might not such a Church actively pursuing social justice on behalf of the oppressed nationalists make the people's perceived need for the use of armed force irrelevant? Would not such a Church following a definite strategy for peace with justice and working for a complete demilitarisation of the north help to resolve the political conflict and thereby bring an end to all political violence?

These are the urgent and challenging questions facing all members of the Catholic Church in Ireland today.

SECTION ONE:

HISTORICAL CONTEXT

CHAPTER I
The Maynooth Factor

'I will be faithful and bear true allegiance to our
most gracious sovereign, Lord King George the Third,
and him will defend to the utmost of my power
against all conspiracies and attempts whatever,
that shall be made against his person, crown and dignity;
and I will to my utmost endeavour to disclose and make known
to his Majesty and heirs, all treasons and traitorous conspiracies
which may be forced against him or them;
and I do faithfully promise to maintain, support and defend
to the utmost of my power, the succession of the crown in his
Majesty's family against any person or persons whatever.'
(OATH OF ALLEGIANCE TO THE BRITISH CROWN TAKEN BY THE STAFF
AND STUDENTS OF MAYNOOTH COLLEGE [1795-1867])

The Catholic Church in Ireland was officially banned under the
Penal Laws, enacted between 1695 and 1727, in the wake of the
defeat of the army of James II by the forces of William of Orange.
Intended to marginalise Catholics politically, socially and
economically, these laws restricted land ownership as well as
employment in the public sector. Catholics could neither vote nor
be elected to parliament, nor could they join the legal profession.
A reward of £5 was placed on the head of a Catholic priest. Those
captured were punished, many by death. Catholic education of
any kind was forbidden and it was illegal for Catholics to send
their children abroad for education.

The Penal Laws were part of the British colonial strategy of
dividing the Irish nation along religious lines:[1]

> all the Protestants on the favourable side of the line, all the
> Catholics on the other side so that the two might never
> again unite. The Lord Chief Justices in 1715 urged upon
> the wholly Protestant Irish Parliament a unanimity among
> the various Protestant sects as 'may once more put an end
> to all other distinctions in Ireland but that of Protestant and
> Papist.'

That unity of Protestants was not to happen for some time yet as the aristocracy which ruled the country on behalf of the British belonged to the Established Church and were not prepared to accept or share with Presbyterians.

However, the extent to which the repressive laws against Catholics were enforced varied from place to place according to the make-up of the local population.[2] In the southern counties of Munster and South Leinster, where the population was overwhelmingly Catholic, the laws had only a limited impact. In such areas a Catholic gentry provided protection for their co-religionists, sometimes holding on to their lands and properties by a tactical conversion to the Protestant faith. By contrast, in Ulster where land and power rested in the hands of a Protestant ascendancy, there was no escaping the full rigour of the laws.

Bishop Hugh McMahon of Clogher, in an official report to the Vatican in 1714, has left us a vivid account of the effect of the Penal Laws on his ministry:

> I frequently had to assume a fictitious name and travel in disguise lest I should be detected by the guards... Although all Ireland is suffering this province is worse off than the rest of the country because of the fact that from the neighbouring country of Scotland, Calvinists are coming over here daily in large groups of families occupying the towns and villages, seizing the farms in richer parts of the country and expelling the natives... The result is that the Catholic natives were forced to build their huts in mountainous or marshy country. Hence, the faithful who in times past have contributed so generously to the support of their clergy, are now themselves in dire poverty and quite unable to help...
>
> To hear Mass the people must rise early and travel through frost and snow: some, many of them in advanced years, leave their homes the previous day to make sure they will arrive in time at the place where Mass is to be celebrated... All who refused the Oath (of allegiance to a Protestant sovereign) were forbidden all practice of religion, and power was given to every magistrate to compel anybody — even people they met on the road — to declare on oath whether they had heard Mass within a given time and, if so, where they heard Mass, who was the celebrant and who was present...

From that time the open practice of religion either ceased entirely or was considerably curtailed according as the persecution varied in intensity. During these years a person was afraid to trust his neighbour lest, being compelled to swear, he might divulge the names of those present at Mass. Moreover, spies are continually moving around posing as Catholics... Greater danger, of course, threatened the priest, as the government persecuted them unceasingly and bitterly, with the result that priests have celebrated Mass with their faces veiled, lest they should be recognised by those present. At other times Mass was celebrated in a closed room with only a server present, the window being left open so that those outside might hear the voice of the priest without knowing who it was, or at least without seeing him...

Over the countryside people might be seen on meeting, signalling to each other on their fingers the hour Mass was due to begin, in order that people might be able to kneel down and follow mentally the Mass which was celebrated at a distance. I myself have often celebrated Mass at night with only the man of the house and his wife present. They were afraid to admit even their children, so fearful were they. The penalty for anyone allowing Mass to be celebrated in his house is a fine of £30 [equivalent to £30,000 today] and imprisonment for a year...[3]

This firsthand account shows how far the British government was prepared to go in its efforts to maintain a Protestant ascendancy which, they believed, would best guarantee and protect their colonial interests in Ireland. The objective of their strategy was described as the creation of a 'Protestant garrison... in possession of the land, magistracy and power of the country: holding their property under the tenure of British power and supremacy, and ready at every instant to crush the rising of the conquered.'[4]

Yet in the latter years of the eighteenth century, the Catholic Church, through the bishops, clergy and wealthy laity who had taken over the Church, had attained a position of power and social respectability which would have been unimaginable a generation earlier. This was particularly so in the southern counties of Ireland where, even in the period of the Penal Laws, 'rich Catholics were quietly tolerated, and generally received from the rich Protestants an amount of respect and forbearance which the latter would not at any time extend to their Protestant tenantry or work-people'.[5]

This class solidarity could be seen at the funeral in 1796 of Bishop Egan of Waterford and Lismore. According to his friend, Bishop Moylan of Cork:

> Nothing could surpass the respect paid by all denominations of people to the memory of our dear friend. The funeral procession was attended by the principal Protestant gentlemen of the county, with the mayor and corporation of Clonmel... Most of the lawyers then on circuit attended and the Judge declared that if he could with propriety quit the bench, he would attend the funeral of so venerable a member of society.[6]

It was class solidarity which led to the emergence of the Catholic Church as a social power. However, the impetus for change came from two distinct developments; firstly, the recognition by the British government that Jacobinism could no longer be regarded as a serious threat; and secondly, the emergence of a socially-radical movement within Europe which was feared by the British government and the Vatican alike. Both were drawn together in opposition to what they considered a common enemy.

The Prefect of Propaganda Fidei in Rome, Cardinal Leonardo Antonelli, devoted much time and energy to cultivating good relations between the Irish Catholic Church's leaders and the English monarchy. In 1778 he exhorted Dr Troy, then Bishop of Ossory, and his fellow bishops 'to pay due respect to the British government and show themselves to be obedient servants, zealous for the good of the state and the prosperity of the sovereign'.[7] The Irish bishops accepted Antonelli's directive, possibly because they recognised that such a course was the only way to avoid further persecution, and his views were reflected in their pastorals.

The bishops had the opportunity to demonstrate their allegiance during the agrarian disturbances of the 1760s and 1770s when the Whiteboys and other agrarian secret societies challenged the oppressive power of landlordism. It was a period of extreme rural poverty and recurring famine, caused to a great extent by the twin evils of absentee landlordism and grasping agents. The Whiteboys organised attacks on guilty landlords, whether Protestant or Catholic, and threatened those who evicted or 'rack-rented' poor tenants or who privatised previously communal land. They also criticised those Catholic clergy, who they felt were exploiting the poor by over-charging for clerical duties.

In 1779, in line with the hierarchy's enthusiastic condemnations of agrarian societies, Dr Troy issued an excommunication order against the Whiteboys:

> Whereas several disorderly persons of our communion and of this diocese, distinguished by the appellation and appearance of White Boys, continue to disturb the public peace and injure private property, notwithstanding the censures of the Church and rigour of the laws against riotous assemblies of any kind... We have from these sacred altars repeatedly explained their duty towards God and the Powers He has appointed to rule over them... We have likewise announced the vengeance of heaven against those unthinking wretches, their associates and abettors and declare them unworthy of the Sacraments and Christian burial... Authorised then as we are by the precepts of Our Lord and His Apostles, we have resolved after mature deliberation and imploring the assistance of heaven, to use the sword of excommunication, and cut off from the Church these rotten and incurable limbs, lest the other members of the Mystical Body should be poisoned or infected by a further communication with them.[8]

In a lengthy address to the four archbishops of Ireland in June 1791, Cardinal Antonelli outlined the religious duty of obedience to 'the legitimate government of George III',[9] and recalling the words of Pope Benedict XIV, he 'urged that those who do not accept the institutions of the State should be punished'.[10] The result of this instruction could be seen when, in December 1793, the Catholic hierarchy of Ireland presented Lord Lieutenant Westmoreland with an address of loyalty to George III and an accompanying letter deploring the lawlessness of 'the lower class of Catholics'.[11] Antonelli reiterated the Vatican policy which forbade 'any union of Catholics and Presbyterians against the secular authority' in a letter to the then Archbishop, Troy, in December 1791.[12] Such correspondence played into the hands of the British authorities who used it to stir up sectarian division, especially in the northern counties. In all their colonies it has been a deliberate policy of the British to play off two religious or ethnic communities against each other.

Diplomatic relations between Britain and Rome were steadily strengthening. The British representative, Sir John Cox Hippisley, had a large circle of friends at the Vatican, one of whom was Monsignor Erskine who was responsible for English and Irish affairs. When Hippisley announced Erskine's arrival in London on 7 September, 1793, the first matter he had to negotiate was the establishment of a national seminary for Ireland, a matter which was already occupying the Irish bishops in their discussions with British officials. As a result of these negotiations, Archbishop Troy on 14 January, 1794, presented 'a memorial' to the British on behalf of the Irish bishops, explaining that under previous legislation the bishops had been forced to send priests abroad for training, usually to France, but that since the revolution this was no longer possible or desirable. Pointing out that the clergy had been complimented more than once 'for assiduously instructing their people in the precepts of charity, for inculcating obedience to the laws and veneration for His Majesty's royal person and government',[13] the report urged the establishment of an Irish seminary for priests, 'lest they might be contaminated by the contagion of sedition and infidelity, and thus become the means of introducing into this country the pernicious maxims of a licentious philosophy.'[14]

A month later, on 17 February, 1794, Monsignor Erskine was able to report that the British government intended 'to erect and endow a seminary for Irish Catholic priests at a cost of £24,000 sterling annually'.[15] In return he had promised the Home Office in London that he would use all his influence with the bishops so that they might instil in their people loyalty and obedience. Furthermore, all staff and students at the new college in Maynooth were required to swear an oath of allegiance to the crown. The opening of the Royal College of Maynooth was seen by both the British and Catholic authorities as a significant step on the road to building a new alliance between Church and State. Conscious of the strong bond of the Irish people to their religion, the British recognised the potential of the 'moral police force'. They were reminded of this potential by the Catholic orator, Richard Lalor Shiel, during a Westminster debate in 1845 on the renewal of the Maynooth grant:

> You must not take the Catholic clergy into your pay, but you can take the Catholic clergy into your care... Are not

lectures at Maynooth cheaper than state prosecutions? Are not professors less costly than crown solicitors? Is not a large standing army and a great constabulary more expensive than the moral police force with which the priesthood of Ireland can be thriftily and efficaciously supplied?

* * * * *

The extent to which the Irish Catholic hierarchy and the clergy as a whole had been imbued with anti-revolutionary feeling was demonstrated when they denounced the rebellion of the United Irishmen in a pastoral read from all the pulpits on 28 May 1798. A month earlier, on the eve of the rebellion, Monsignor Erskine, writing to Archbishop Troy, reiterated that the people were duty bound to obey the civil authority. Was it possible, he asked, referring to the United Irishmen, that Irish Catholics who 'for centuries have withstood all temptations and hardships not to forsake the religion of their forefathers and the duties inseparable from it, should now have given way to the insinuations of designing persons and think of joining hands with the declared enemies of religion?'[16] He urged the Archbishop: 'Make use of all the means that your situation affords you to open the eyes of deluded people; sermons, exhortations, confessions, prayers'.[17] Within two days of the reading of the pastoral, Lord Lieutenant Cornwallis received an address of loyalty signed by all the Irish bishops, the President of Maynooth, and other leading clergy and laity. The entire Catholic Establishment had united in opposition to the union of Catholic, Protestant and Dissenter in the revolutionary struggle for Irish freedom.

The diverging attitude of the Catholic hierarchy and a section of the Catholic people was nowhere more pronounced than in County Wexford which was to become a principal flashpoint in the United Irishmen Rebellion. There a situation had evolved where two political groups appealed for the support of the Catholic masses. The moderate, pro-establishment Catholic group which owned property favoured a conservative image; Bishop Caulfield of Ferns was typical of this group. The other, made up of younger, politically more aggressive Catholics, agitated for the advancement of Catholics on all fronts; legal, social, economic and political. This group was anti-government and anti-establishment, and from it came the leadership of the United Irishmen in Wexford.

Seeing them as being 'fatally influenced' by the French revolutionary movement,[18] Bishop Caulfield was virulently opposed to the radical politics of the younger group. He accused them of being 'anti-clerical' and he denounced those priests who supported the movement.[19] His conservative views were reflected by most of the senior clergy in the diocese who were totally opposed to the radicalism of the few priests who subsequently supported the rebellion. Typical of this conservative group was John Shallow, parish priest of Adamstown, who on seeing the advances being made by the United Irishmen in his parish, 'did combat and deprecate them... from my altar as also in private, as analogous to, and flowing from, French atheistical revolutionary principles, and derogating from, and repugnant to, the established laws of the land and the law of God...'[20] He did his best to inculcate in his people 'obedience to their beloved sovereign, King George the Third, for the many favours he bestowed on them and the gratitude they in consequence owed him'.[21] Fr Francis Kavanagh, the vicar-general of the diocese of Ferns, stated that in the year prior to the rebellion he had 'uniformly reprobated the proceedings of the United Irishmen as tending not only to disunion amongst fellow subjects but to disloyalty and sedition.'[22] Many priests allowed magistrates to speak from their altars in a bid to keep their parishes quiescent; others collaborated in the search for arms; another, John Redmond of Camolin, deliberately turned away United Irishmen from their Easter duty in the months prior to the rebellion.

The Catholic clergy opposed the United Irishmen on a number of distinct grounds. Firstly, they were condemned as a 'secret society', and therefore, not sanctioned by lawful authority. Secondly, they were unacceptable in that they were inspired by 'atheistic principles'. Thirdly, they were opposed on political grounds by those who argued that a low-key, constitutional approach was the best way to win concessions. Then there was the argument that the United Irishmen were divisive and destroyed the natural links between the clergy and the people, substituting anarchy in its place. And, of course, there was the theory that the entire rebellion was the result of a conspiracy by a 'small self-serving group of criminals.'[23]

THE MAYNOOTH FACTOR   23

Bishop Caulfield summarised the attitude of senior Churchmen:

> The uniting of Irishmen for the late rebellion was hatched in the dark, or was communicated by private whispers; it was recommended by specious promises, impressed by flattering prospects, enforced by threats and menaces, denouncing death and destruction on the persons and properties of those who refused to unite and to co-operate, and the union was secured and sanctioned by a solemn oath. The people, in general more credulous than wise or virtuous, swallowed the bait and joined in the diabolical confederacy, adhering to their perjurous oaths more strictly than to their baptismal vows, or the most sacred ties of conscience, religion and the word of God. All this accumulation of misfortunes was brought on the country by the machinations of crazy, ambitious, revolutionary adventurers, through the credulity of the incautious and ignorant multitude.[24]

Those ten or so priests from Wexford who joined in the rebellion were duly punished. Six were suspended from their ministry; the others, reprimanded. Father Murphy of Boolevogue was executed by the British. The vast majority of clergy, however, stood with the British, many of them organising displays of public loyalty such as that presented by the Reverend Edan Murphy and 514 parishioners of the parish of Kilrush:

> We, the RC inhabitants of Kilrush in the County of Wexford this day assembled at the chapel of Kilrush, holding in abhorrence the barbarous outrages lately committed and seditious conspiracies now existing in this Kingdom by traitors and rebels styling themselves United Irishmen, consider it incumbent on us thus to vow and declare our unalterable attachment and loyalty to our beloved Sovereign King George III and our determined resolution to support and maintain his rights and our happy Constitution... and we do pledge ourselves to co-operate with our Protestant brethren of this Kingdom in opposing, to the utmost of our power, any foreign or domestic enemy who may dare to invade his dominion or to disturb the peace and tranquillity of this country.[25]

The Catholic Church leadership responded as the British had hoped and expected. This was hardly surprising, given the social background of its chief leaders, including Archbishop Troy and Bishop Moylan of Cork, who were described by one commentator as 'men of the Pale by birth and therefore, favourable to English rule, in spite of its tyranny and oppression. Both were educated on the Continent at a time when passive obedience and the divine right of kings were taught in all their ethical and theological treatises.'[26] Bishop Moylan, 'a thorough-going loyalist',[27] urged the people of Cork to be passive in recognition of the 'advantages of British rule', which he declared 'should excite and call forth our gratitude...' to be demonstrated by 'unshaken loyalty to our gracious Sovereign — a Sovereign who had done more for the Roman Catholic Body and indeed the Kingdom in general, than any of his predecessors.'[28] His pastoral, dated 26 April, 1798, was addressed to his 'beloved flock' and 'in particular to the lower order of the RC inhabitants of the diocese of Cork.'[29]

The official historian of Maynooth College, Dr Healy, remarked that both the trustees and staff were 'eminently loyal'.[30] Referring to a report, current during the rebellion, that some students were involved, he stated: 'As a result all of the students were questioned about their allegiances'.[31] Ten were expelled immediately; seven others later. One of the expelled students, called Hearne, was executed for participation in the rebellion. Dr Healy reports that 'it was stated in the *Dublin Journal* at the time that "great intercession had been made by the Roman Catholic clergy of this city to save the life of Hearne..." This paragraph was copied into *The Sun* and other English newspapers, giving rise to much prejudice both against the college and the Catholic clergy of the city of Dublin.'[32] Dr Healy noted that Dr Troy, writing to the under-secretary, Mr Marshall, declared the statement 'entirely false',[33] and stated that Hearne 'was not a student at Maynooth when engaged in seditious practices.'[34] According to Dr Healy: 'Dr Troy called for a formal contradiction of the paragraph the effect of which was "to represent the clergy of this city and I, as their head, as abettors of treason and Maynooth College as a nursery of traitors."' The offending paragraph was withdrawn.[35]

Dr Healy also states that when an attempt was made to withdraw funding for Maynooth, 'Lord Cornwallis remonstrated with the Lord Chancellor who, in his reply, declared that his purpose was not to destroy the College which he considered to be

THE MAYNOOTH FACTOR   25

now a great national object, essential to the public security.'[36]

The 1798 Rebellion was defeated by the military might of the British state and its allies in Ireland, amongst whom were numbered the Catholic hierarchy and most clergy. Like the British government, the landlords and the entire Protestant ascendancy, they were determined to hold firm against the revolutionary ideas of a movement which they perceived as a threat to their power. The suppression of the rebellion resulted in the loss of an estimated 40,000 lives.

As it entered the nineteenth century, the Catholic Church in Ireland attained a position of power, control and social 'respectability' which would have been unimaginable during the era of the Penal Laws. However, the moral authority which it had gained from its social alignment with the poor and oppressed during that era was lost. In opposing the United Irishmen Rebellion, they had aligned themselves with the status quo — a corrupt, vicious, colonial regime — against their own oppressed congregations.

The real winner in all of this was the British government which set about completing the conquest of Ireland, secure in the knowledge that the leadership of the Catholic Church would act as a buffer between their misrule and the organised revolutionary resistance of an oppressed people.

CHAPTER 2

The Vatican Influence

*'We have tried to govern Ireland by conciliation and have failed also.
No other means are now open to us except those we are resolved on
using, namely, to govern Ireland through Rome.'*
(BRITISH PRIME MINISTER, LORD JOHN RUSSELL [1792-1878])

The new century began with the passing of the Act of Union in
June 1800, a measure that ended the limited self-government
which had been enjoyed by the Irish Protestant ascendancy. The
change was welcomed by individual members of the Catholic
hierarchy, amongst them Bishop Moylan of Cork:[1]

> Nothing in my opinion will more effectually tend to lay
> those disgraceful and scandalous party feuds and
> dissensions, and restore peace and harmony amongst us,
> than that great measure in contemplation of the legislative
> Union and Incorporation of this Kingdom with Great
> Britain...

However, the 'peace and harmony' of even closer union with
Britain did not satisfy the remnants of the United Irishmen who, in
1803, rose in a short-lived rebellion under the leadership of Robert
Emmet. Once again, the bishops rushed to support the government. The Bishop of Cloyne, Dr Coppinger, issued a pastoral
denouncing those involved:

> The most inattentive among us cannot but be struck with
> the fate of these infatuated people who have allowed
> themselves to be deceived by the empty sound of Gallic
> (French) liberty and Gallic equality, the treacherous
> passwords employed by hell against the altar, the throne
> and the peace of society.

Archbishop Troy wrote to Sir John Cox Hippisley, the British
representative at the Vatican, enclosing a brochure in which he
condemned Emmet's rebellion and quoted the newly-inserted

questions in the Catechism which Hippisley himself had recommended. These took the form of an appendix to Lesson 17 on the Fourth Commandment:[2]

Q. What are the duties of subjects to the temporal powers?

A. To be subject to them and to honour and obey them not only for wrath but also for conscience sake; for so is the will of God (Peter 2; Romans 13).

Q. Does the Scripture require any other duty of subjects?

A. Yes, to pray for Kings and for all who are in high station that we may lead a quiet and peaceful life (2 Timothy 2).

Q. Is it sinful to resist or combine against the established authorities or to speak with contempt or disregard of those who rule over us?

A. Yes, St Paul says let every soul be subject to higher powers; he that resisteth the power, resisteth the ordnances of God; and they that resist, purchase to themselves damnation. (Romans 13).

* * * * *

The relaxation of the Penal Laws towards the end of the eighteenth century had allowed the emergence of a Catholic professional and merchant class. It was from the ranks of this emerging middle class that the diocesan clergy of the nineteenth century were largely recruited. In the words of Dr Crotty, President of Maynooth College, his students were:[3]

> generally the sons of farmers who must be comfortable in order to meet the expenses, of tradesmen, shopkeepers and not a very small proportion of them are the children of opulent merchants and rich farmers and graziers... the students overwhelmingly came from what in Ireland is considered the middling class.

By the early decades of the century it had become apparent that, apart from the north-east, the Act of Union was an unmitigated disaster for native commerce which had been placed at a severe disadvantage in relation to British manufactures. The 'middling class' grew increasingly restive and more assertive in voicing its concerns. To the annoyance of the hierarchy and of the British government, the clergy began to reflect those concerns. As early as 1815, when the ending of the Napoleonic Wars led to a drastic fall in prices for agricultural produce, the discontent of the large farmers and graziers was being echoed in the ranks of the clergy. In response, the British turned to Rome for help and the Vatican duly issued a call to its clergy in Ireland to stay out of politics.

But the movement for change could not be stopped so easily, and even though the Statutes of Maynooth ensured that its students were reminded that 'no power or authority could release them from their duty to obey the King' this did not rule out support for some limited form of self-government which would be to the economic advantage of their class.[4] Thus was seen the emergence of 'constitutional nationalism', under the leadership of Daniel O'Connell and supported, by and large, by the Catholic clergy.

Under the auspices of the Catholic Association founded in 1823, O'Connell led a campaign for Catholic Emancipation from the remaining Penal Laws which would give Catholics the right to go to Westminster. The clergy were closely involved in the campaign and they, in turn, enlisted the support of the poor who were asked to pay one penny a month to help maintain it. Within six years the campaign had proved successful, the Catholic Relief Act being passed in 1829.

Further campaigns followed, of resistance to the payment of tithes to the Protestant Church and for the repeal of the Act of Union. As in 1815, the British turned to Rome and to the Irish hierarchy for help in halting clerical involvement in politics. In January 1834, the entire hierarchy at a synod in Dublin passed two resolutions unanimously, one repeating in stronger terms an injunction of 1830 that priests stay clear of politics and concern themselves solely with their spiritual vocations, and the other making generally applicable throughout Ireland the Leinster bishops' prohibition on the use of ecclesiastical buildings for any secular purpose, 'except in cases connected with charity or religion.'[5]

Also in 1834, the British government intervened when a new Archbishop was to be appointed to the Archdiocese of Tuam. They called on the Pope not to appoint 'an agitating prelate', referring to Bishop John MacHale of Killala who had supported O'Connell's emancipation movement.[6] Pope Gregory XVI ignored their request on this occasion and appointed MacHale to the position. British pressure continued, however, and in the spring of 1839 the Vatican's Prefect of Propaganda Fidei, Cardinal Fransoni, wrote two private letters to the Irish Primate, Dr Crolly, concerning reports that 'MacHale and the other Irish bishops were presiding over political banquets denouncing the government and exciting popular passions.'[7] Dr Crolly was instructed to dissuade them 'not only from all political activity but from even all semblance of political involvement.'[8] The contents of these letters were communicated to all the Irish bishops but had no immediate effect. As Dr Crolly replied to Cardinal Fransoni, the Irish hierarchy had to exercise 'the greatest prudence... lest we offend a faithful people by an unexpected separation from them.'[9]

In 1844, the British government persuaded the Vatican to reprimand the Irish clergy again, this time quite publicly. The Pope's rescript of that year was severe. It complained that the Fransoni injunction of 1839 had been ignored, 'to the discredit as well as the sorrow of the Holy See'.[10] Ecclesiastics were sternly reminded of their sacred duty to 'separate themselves from all secular concerns and by work and example to inculcate subjection to the temporal power in civil matters and to dissipate popular excitements.'[11] Dr Crolly was instructed to admonish all ecclesiastics, especially bishops, who defied this teaching.

A year later, in an attempt to defuse the Repeal campaign, the Peel administration at Westminster made a substantial increase in the grant to Maynooth College. Furthermore, in keeping with its policy that the Catholic Church would have the task 'of civilising and socially controlling the Irish people',[12] the British considered giving the Church complete control of the education of Catholic children under the National School System which had been set up and financed by the British government since 1831.

When Lord John Russell became Prime Minister of Britain in 1846, and Pius IX succeeded Gregory XVI as Pope in the same year, a new period in Westminster/Vatican diplomacy began. Russell immediately dispatched his father-in-law, the Earl of Minto, to Rome to build up stronger and closer ties with the Vatican. As the Repeal movement reached its zenith, with mass public demonstrations, the viceroy in Ireland declared: 'At no period in

Irish history has the soothing influence of religion been more required than at the present moment.'[13]

Lord Clarendon developed this point in a memorandum:

> Among the social influences may be placed foremost the strong religious feelings which exist in the Roman Catholic people generally for Ecclesiastical authority and which would, beyond doubt, make them as a mass shrink from opposing any decided act of authority on the part of the Pope as if they were committing a sacrilege... Instructions should be issued by His Holiness to the Archbishops and Bishops of Ireland to prohibit the clergy under pains and penalties from attending political meetings or joining political movements either by becoming subscribers or members or otherwise and that restrictions should, of course, extend to the prelates themselves.[14]

Prime Minister Russell accepted that 'no other means are now open to us except those that we are resolved on using, namely to govern Ireland through Rome.'[15] He dispatched Minto to the Vatican with clear instructions which were outlined to Queen Victoria by Foreign Secretary, Lord Palmerston:

> While on the one hand he holds out to the Pope the support and protection which the countenance and good offices of the British government will afford, Lord Minto would endeavour to obtain from the Pope the exertion of his spiritual authority over the Catholic priesthood of Ireland to induce them to abstain from repeal agitation, and to urge them not to embarrass but rather to assist your Majesty's government.[16]

Minto reported back that he had 'found no difficulty' with Pius IX and that 'we were to expect from him the assistance of his authority if needed' to 'restrain' the Catholic Church in Ireland.[17] Shortly after the Minto mission, the Pope issued a renewed call to the Irish bishops and clergy to abstain from political activity. By then, however, the Repeal movement was already running out of steam, through lack of decisiveness on the part of its leadership and because it was overshadowed by the mass human suffering of the Great Famine.

Famine was a recurring fact of life for the mass of the Irish people who lived in conditions of extreme poverty and for whom neither Catholic Emancipation nor the objectives of the Repeal movement were of any material benefit. The poor had known serious famine in 1817 and again in the years 1821-22, though there was no shortage of food in the country. Agrarian secret societies continued to struggle against the injustices which led to such misery. Between 1800 and 1833, there were 114 parliamentary commissions and 60 select committees established to investigate rural agitation, but no reforms were ever introduced and the situation of a rapidly-expanding population steadily deteriorated. In the Great Famine of the 1840s an estimated one million people died and millions more were forced to emigrate. Those who suffered were the labourers, cottiers and small farmers who comprised the bulk of the population.

The strong farmers of the south and east were largely unaffected by the tragedy, while the stronger tenant farmers in the areas worst affected were able to increase their holdings and their social power. As a result the middle class and larger tenant farmers constituted a greater and more powerful element in Irish society than in pre-Famine days. Together they formed a socially-conservative grouping which was, in effect, the mainstay of the Catholic Church as it entered the latter half of the century.

* * * * *

The most influential Irish Catholic churchman of the century was appointed to Armagh Archdiocese in 1850. Paul Cullen had been rector of the Irish College in Rome since 1832. A highly-conservative man, he was moved to the Dublin Archdiocese in 1852, and in 1866 became the first Irish Cardinal. He ushered in an era of church-building and the acquisition of property. At the Synod of Thurles in 1850, he proposed a resolution that the bishops would demand rather than request complete control of the National School System.

By the end of the century the Church not only controlled the existing system of public education but determined the course of any future developments as well. This extension of the Church's 'social control' may not have been the guarantee against rebellion that the British would have liked, but it ensured the continued hostility of the Church leadership towards any revolutionary movement that might threaten the status quo. Like so many of the hierarchy before him, Cardinal Cullen was to prove himself an inveterate opponent of the forces of militant nationalism.

His first encounter was with remaining members of the Young Ireland movement who had staged an abortive attempt at revolution in 1848. Cardinal Cullen had not been in Ireland at the time of the revolt, but he was Archbishop of Dublin in 1861 when the remains of the veteran Young Irelander, Terence Bellew McManus, were brought back to the city from California where he had died in exile. Cardinal Cullen refused to allow the remains into any Church building for a funeral service. The body was taken to the Mechanics Institute instead and a burial service conducted by a Fr Patrick Lavelle. Fr Lavelle was subsequently suspended from the ministry in 1864. Cardinal Cullen wrote of the affair in a letter dated 10 November, 1861:

> Some lunatic decided to bring the remains home to arouse a revolutionary spirit and a committee of Protestants, Catholics and the people of no religion was formed... There was a large funeral, mostly artisans and mechanics; the Catholics of standing abstained.

In a further letter, dated 29 November, 1861, Cullen stated that he could not have acted differently given that the funeral was intended 'as a declaration in favour of the rebellion of 1848', and had he allowed it, he would have been 'giving sanction to revolutionary principles which are destroying religion everywhere they prevail'. A few years later he was to become even more strident in his condemnations of the Fenian movement. On 10 October 1865, he stated: 'All who join in such societies are excommunicated and cannot be absolved as long as they continue connected with them.' He also called the Fenian rebellion a 'compound of folly and wickedness, wearing the mask of patriotism to make dupes of the unwary... the work of a few fanatics.'[18]

The deep division which existed between the Church hierarchy and the Irish revolutionary movement was evident when a Fenian newspaper, *The Irish People*, challenged the clerical intervention in politics: 'We saw from the first that ecclesiastical authority in temporal affairs should be shivered to atoms before we could advance a single step towards the liberation of our suffering country.'[19] A swift response came from Bishop Moriarity of Kerry who, speaking from the pulpit of Killarney Cathedral, denounced the Fenians:

> Oh God's heaviest curse, his withering blighting, blasting curse on them... When we look down into the fathomless depth of this infamy of the leaders of the Fenian Conspiracy, we must acknowledge that eternity is not long enough, nor hell hot enough to punish such miscreants.[20]

Other bishops appealed for moderation and called for support for constitutionalism. They accepted that injustices existed but said the only way to get rid of them was to appeal to the English sense of 'fair play'. On 23 March, 1867, newspapers reported an address by Archbishop Leahy of Cashel, asking the people to:

> trust that the growing liberality of the statesmen of England and the sense of justice as well as the sympathies of the English people should bring about the redress of our grievances, not by an appeal to arms but by peaceable constitutional means which all good men can approve and which deserve the benison of heaven.

Condemnation of the Fenians by the bishops was echoed by the vast bulk of the clergy. A *Guardian Report* of February 1866 stated that 'the priests are denouncing Fenianism on every side and warning their flocks against it.' The British were pleased at the response of the Church as was shown in a letter sent by the viceroy, Lord Spencer, to the home secretary, Lord Clarendon, on 21 December, 1869:

> Since we have been in office many RC clergy have given support to the government against Fenianism and agrarian outrage. Foremost among these have been Cardinal Cullen and Archbishop Leahy of Cashel. They both issued strong pastorals against Fenianism and agrarian crime. Other bishops have acted in the same spirit, Bishop Moriarity among them. There have been, however, some very strong speeches and letters written by priests which have indirectly encouraged crime and sedition, though they have not actually transgressed the law. I am happy to say that in the last week two of those who made themselves conspicuous have been suspended — Father Ryan and Father Mooney...[21]

The Pope also added his voice to the condemnation of the Fenians. In response to a request from the Irish bishops who were in Rome for the First Vatican Council, he issued a statement through the Holy Office of the Inquisition on 12 January, 1870.[22]

*　*　*　*　*

With the collapse of the Fenian Rising and its leaders in jail or in exile, the hope of setting up an Irish Republic faded. However, on their release from prison some of the Fenians regrouped to organise a Land League campaign aimed at overthrowing the evil of landlordism. The main impetus for such a campaign came from a former Fenian, Michael Davitt, who was released from jail in December 1877. He sought and received the support of Charles Stewart Parnell, the emerging leader of constitutional nationalism. By September 1879, the Land League had established branches throughout Ireland with the support of the tenant farmers.

With two notable exceptions, Dr Croke, Archbishop of Cashel, and Dr Nulty, Bishop of Meath, the main body of the Catholic hierarchy, led by Archbishop McCabe of Dublin, united to oppose the Land League. However, the League won widespread support from the parochial clergy, most of whom came from a farming background and who, therefore, were in sympathy with the plight of the tenant farmers. Priests became active in local committees, a fact which caused the Vatican and the British much concern, just as similar involvement with the Repeal movement a generation earlier had done.

Archbishop McCabe attacked the Land League repeatedly and sought the support of Rome. Dr Croke poured scorn on what he described as the 'peculiar political theories' of the Dublin Archbishop.[23] In a letter to the Rector of the Irish College in Rome, he wrote that to follow the advice of Archbishop McCabe would bring ruin on the Church. He added that the Archbishop:

> has got himself applauded to the skies by the Orange Press of Ireland and the Tory Press of England...I suppose in his communications with Rome he did not tell you that for the first time in Ireland's history an Irish bishop had been served with threatening notices that he would be shot — a fact which he mentioned to me with his own lips.[24]

In a later correspondence, Dr Croke warned that 'if Rome keeps interfering in Irish politics or if it gets publicly and generally known that the Roman authorities side with those who have gone by word and deed against the public, papal influence in Ireland will fall as low as it is in France and Italy.'[25] In the end, however, pressure from Rome forced Dr Croke to offer an apology to Archbishop McCabe, and in 1882, the Dublin Archbishop received his Cardinal's hat, an indication of Rome's support.

The Land League campaign continued, meanwhile, and had some success in forcing the British to introduce reforms, even if in tandem with new coercive legislation. So successful was the movement in mobilising public support that Parnell proceeded to build a mass campaign for Home Rule, a programme for limited self-government. In October 1882, the Irish National League was formed to secure this objective. Three years later, in the 1885 general election, Parnell's party secured the balance of power at Westminster. This success was followed by a Plan of Campaign against rent arrears, during which fourteen priests were jailed and the British government seriously considered prosecuting Dr Croke.

In 1888, the Holy See again intervened, issuing a Papal Rescript which condemned the Plan of Campaign. Dr Croke wrote again to the Rector of the Irish College in Rome informing him that Pope Leo XIII is 'cursed in every mood and tense from Donegal to Baltimore and, where his picture was found in private homes, it was either being displaced or torn to bits.'[26] But in 1890, as news broke of Parnell's involvement in a divorce case, the conservative views of the majority of the hierarchy were reasserted in a manifesto condemning the man who had been popularly titled 'the uncrowned King of Ireland'.

Parnell died in 1891 and with him died the possibility of meaningful reforms being forced from the British by the combined power of the constitutional and militant strands of Irish nationalism. There had been achievements, however, including the undermining of the power of the landlords, and many clergy had played a part in that victory despite the official view of their bishops. In a letter to Dr Croke a few days before he died on 14 August, 1896, Dr Duggan the Bishop of Clonfert congratulated him for the stance he had adopted in the Land War. He commented: 'Never fall out with the extreme men because you will find in due course that they are often extremely right.'[27]

By the close of the nineteenth century, the Catholic Church, strongest in the southern counties, was a powerful and socially-conservative force in Irish society. While its leaders were overwhelmingly pro-British in their outlook, the bulk of the clergy mirrored the interests of the middle class and tenant farmers from which they were mainly recruited. Like Dr Croke, they saw the danger in the Church opposing popular opinion and so they developed a certain pragmatism in relation to political affairs. They were never revolutionary but they recognised the strength of the folk culture which is based in the revolutionary tradition. Being pragmatists, it was no surprise then to see the Church leaders play a leading role in centenary celebrations to mark the United Irishmen Rebellion of 1798. There were further revolutions to come as the Church entered the twentieth century.

CHAPTER 3

The Catholic Hierarchy and Partition

'If the bishops had to choose between accepting the northern state and losing their schools then they were going to keep their schools.'
(MICHAEL FARRELL, *Northern Ireland:The Orange State*)

The British conquest of Ireland was virtually complete by the early years of the twentieth century. The process of colonisation by the English government had nearly destroyed the distinctive Irish culture, particularly in the larger towns and cities where British royalty received the same welcome they might have expected in an English city. On the surface at least, it appeared that the Irish revolution was defeated, and that the most the Irish people wanted was the limited self-government of 'home rule' being pursued by the Irish Parliamentary Party.

There was, however, an undercurrent of activity by a 'despised and slandered minority' in a number of social, cultural and political organisations. It was amongst such dissident elements that the revolutionary spirit was fostered by an emerging generation of Irish radicals. The new radicalism could be seen in the efforts of socialist leaders, such as James Connolly and Jim Larkin, to challenge the injustices which forced the urban and rural working class to live in conditions of abject poverty. Trade unionism flourished in the face of bitter opposition from the employers and their establishment allies, amongst them the Catholic hierarchy. When the employers locked out their workers in August 1913 in an attempt to smash the union, and when the police then baton-charged protests by workers on the streets of Dublin, the Church authorities showed where their allegiance lay. Archbishop Walsh of Dublin received a report from his secretary on the situation: 'It is simply the scum of our slums versus the police... I think it is a scandal that the military have not been utilised... any person who got batoned richly deserved it.'[1]

Towards the end of October 1913, when many were on the verge of starvation, Archbishop Walsh condemned those Catholic mothers who were going to send their hungry children to the homes of sympathetic socialists in Britain. Reactionary Catholic mobs attacked the organisers of the scheme and physically prevented the children from going. The police intervened and arrested the organisers, charging them with 'kidnapping'.[2] James Connolly, acting general secretary of the Irish Transport and General Workers Union, (ITGWU) challenged the Church authorities by suspending free dinners at Liberty Hall (union headquarters) and sending the women and children to the Archbishop's palace to ask for food. There they were told that 'the dinners are not for Larkin's people'.[3]

The hostility of the Church hierarchy to the trade unions was hardly surprising given, as Jim Larkin pointed out, that seventy priests were among the leading shareholders of the Dublin Tram Company which was at the centre of the dispute. As in the Land Wars, the attitude of the clergy was determined by class alignment rather than by an objective analysis of the rights and wrongs of the situation:

> In the 1880s and 1910s the Church hierarchy and clergy sided with those it was attached to by ties of kinship, financial dependency, common outlook and shared lifestyles. It was not attached in this way to the poor farm labourers or to the unskilled workers in Dublin.[4]

* * * * *

In 1914 the Catholic hierarchy joined with John Redmond, leader of the Irish Parliamentary Party, in encouraging Irish youth to join the British army in the First World War. Two years later, when it was being suggested that the Catholic Church was being less than enthusiastic about the 'war effort', a rebuttal was published by the *Freeman's Journal* in an editorial titled 'Irish Bishops and the War'. The editorial cited various Lenten Pastorals which clearly showed where the hierarchy stood. Cardinal Logue was quoted condemning the murder of civilians by Germans using Zeppelins and submarines. The Archbishop of Tuam was quoted telling his flock that 'the man who strikes a blow against the Prussians strikes a blow for justice, freedom and right', while the Bishop of Clonfert declared that 'England's was a just defence against unwarranted aggression'.[5]

Praising those who had gone to war, the Bishop of Kildare and Leighlin said: 'they are defending the shores of Ireland in the trenches of the continent'. Referring to German militarism as 'the outcome of the new paganism',[6] the Bishop of Raphoe echoed a sentiment of his neighbouring Bishop of Derry, who described alleged German atrocities as 'excesses without parallel even in the pages of pagan history'.[7] These pastoral quotations were incorporated into the recruitment leaflets used by the British army.

A fortnight after the publication of the *Freeman's Journal* editorial, the Catholic hierarchy would once more be making pronouncements on a war involving Britain. The other side of this conflict were not Germans, however, but fellow Irishmen and women, members of various nationalist, socialist and republican organisations which had united in an armed rebellion against British rule. Again, the overwhelming majority of the Catholic hierarchy sided with Britain in condemning the insurgents; only one, Bishop Edward O'Dwyer of Limerick, showed sympathy for the rebels:

> Was I to condemn them? Even if their rebellion was not justifiable theologically, was I to join in the condemnation of Pearse, MacDonagh and Colbert... and the men and women who, without trial, were deported from their country in thousands...? Rebellion to be lawful must be the act of a nation as a whole, but while that is true, see the case of the Irish Volunteers against England. The very government against which they rose, and which dealt with them so mercilessly, has proclaimed its own condemnation. What is that ghost of Home Rule which they keep in lavender on the Statute Book but a confession of the wrong of England's rule in Ireland?[8]

Dr O'Dwyer's was a lone voice. Of the nine bishops whose comments were reported after the rebellion, seven condemned it in the strongest terms, including Cardinal Logue,[9] while an eighth, Dr Fogarty of Killaloe, conceded 'that they died bravely and unselfishly for what they believed — foolishly indeed — was the cause of Ireland'.[10] Cardinal Logue referred to the rebellion as 'a lamentable disturbance',[11] while Bishop Hoare of Ardagh and Clonmacnoise said it was 'a mad and sinful venture'.[12] Bishop Kelly of Ross told his congregation in Skibbereen that on those responsible for organising the rebellion 'was the guilt of murder'. But, Archbishop Harty of Cashel probably summed up the political view of the rebellion from the standpoint of the hierarchy: 'We all know that the people of Ireland do not want revolutionary measures. We are perfectly well aware that the people of Ireland believe that by constitutional means they can obtain substantial redress of their grievances. The history of the past shows that all revolutionary measures are doomed to failure.'

Even as the revolution gained momentum, especially after the general election of 1918, the Church was slow to change its stance. There was no recognition given to Dáil Éireann, the Irish parliament established by the Sinn Féin party which had been given an overwhelming mandate from the electorate, at the expense of the Irish Parliamentary Party. Bishop Cohalan of Cork stated his view clearly: 'The question is: was the proclamation of an Irish Republic by Sinn Féin members of parliament after the last general election sufficient to constitute Ireland a republic according to our Church teaching? I answer it was not.'

Throughout the course of what became known as 'the Tan war', the bishops and clergy issued strong denunciations of the armed struggle being fought by the Irish Republican Army. Bishop Cohalan went a step further by excommunicating Catholics who had any involvement with the IRA, a step lauded by the *London Times* which urged the hierarchy as a whole to follow Dr Cohalan's example. Tom Barry, leader of the IRA in West Cork, wrote of his feelings at the time of the excommunication decree:

> My own reaction was one of anger... For days I brooded over the decree knowing full well how deeply religious the IRA were. However, in the event every active service man in our brigade continued to fight, most priests continued to administer the sacraments and the IRA practised their religion as before.[13]

The other bishops did not go as far as Dr Cohalan. They were not prepared to risk alienating an ever-increasing number of their flock, including many within the middle class, who were being somewhat radicalised by the repressive nature of the British counter-insurgency campaign. Once again, it was as a result of their social alignment with the middle class that the hierarchy issued its most critical pastoral ever on British activity in Ireland following the burning by British troops of business premises in Balbriggan in September 1920.

In the weeks and months following this pastoral, three priests were murdered by British forces, while priests throughout the country were subjected to a great deal of harassment. Some were imprisoned while others were shot at. Archbishop Mannix of Melbourne, an outspoken opponent of Britain, was debarred from entering Ireland.

The Government of Ireland Act was passed by the British in May 1920, in an attempt to restore stability. The Act established two partitioned statelets in Ireland with separate parliaments and a limited degree of self-government. At a meeting in June 1920 the bishops described the Act as a 'sham settlement'[14] and in May 1921, Bishop McRory of Down and Connor had a letter read in all the churches of his diocese, prior to an election to the newly-established Belfast parliament, urging his flock to vote against partition.[15]

Within a year the situation had changed and the Catholic hierarchy became one of the principal supporters of a Treaty settlement which formalised the provisions of the Government of Ireland Act. In this, it was again reflecting the views of the middle class which saw its interests being adequately served under the proposed settlement. Individual elected representatives, opposed to the Treaty during the debate on the issue in Dáil Éireann, came under pressure from bishops and priests to change their minds. And when the Dáil had narrowly passed the measure under Britain's threat of 'immediate and terrible war' if they should reject it, the bishops showed their support for the pro-Treaty lobby — 'The best and wisest course for Ireland is to accept the Treaty and make the most of the freedom it undoubtedly gives us.'[16]

The Church hierarchy gave its unequivocal backing to the emerging Free State administration following its attack on the Republican headquarters in Dublin's Four Courts and in the outright civil war that the attack began. The Belfast-based Catholic Protection Committee spoke for the Bishop of Down and Connor when it sent a message to Dublin within days of the Four Court's attack, congratulating the government 'on the success of its labours for the restoration of peace and good order in Dublin and the country' and wishing it 'God-speed in its efforts.'[17]

A lengthy pastoral was issued in October 1922 by the bishops meeting in Maynooth. Republicans, or 'irregulars' as they were referred to, were put under general excommunication and forbidden the use of the sacraments so long as they continued to 'wage war'. The pastoral which was read from pulpits throughout the country continued:

> The guerrilla warfare now being carried out by the irregulars is without moral sanction and therefore the killing of national soldiers in the course of it is murder before God; the seizing of public and private property is robbery; the breaking of roads, bridges and railways is a criminal destruction; the invasion of homes and the molestation of civilians is a grievous crime.[18]

What effect the pastoral had on Republicans is impossible to say. It may have put pressure on waverers but the attitude of most Republicans was probably summed up in the contemporary taunt: 'May your son be a bishop!'[19] The pastoral's main effect was to give the emerging Free State government the 'moral support' it needed in order to introduce draconian legislation and repressive measures, which even the British had not dared to use.

The Army Powers Resolution, known to Republicans as the Murder Act, was passed on 10 October 1922. Under its terms military tribunals were given power to execute anyone found carrying arms or ammunition; aiding or abetting in attacks, destruction or seizure of property; and indeed, virtually anybody even remotely involved with the Republican side in the civil war. Under this repressive legislation 77 people were summarily executed and as many as 13,000 people were interned in prison camps, disused workhouses, ships and army barracks.[20] There was no condemnation of these tactics from within the ranks of the hierarchy nor from the clergy; the theory of 'guilt by association' being supported by Cardinal Logue himself when he excommunicated the entire population of Carlingford, County Louth, following IRA activity in the locality.

*   *   *   *   *

With the defeat of the Republicans in the civil war, the Catholic hierarchy assumed a major role in determining the social and moral climate within which the Free State was to be governed. This was the antithesis of the non-sectarian pluralism which the revolutionary movement had tried to achieve, and it reinforced the very sectarian divisions which Britain had sought to create in setting up two states on the basis of religious affiliation.

Within the northern, partitioned statelet a pro-British, unionist party began the process of creating 'a Protestant state for a Protestant people' through policies of political, social and economic discrimination.[21] In such circumstances, it might have been expected that the Catholic Church leaders would strenuously oppose the new regime. The reality proved different.

By October 1923, the Church leadership was already urging elected representatives of the Nationalist Party in the six counties to abandon their abstentionist policy in relation to the Belfast parliament and to take their seats in defence of 'Catholic interests'.[22] The reason for the hierarchy's action was the proposed change in the education system which would have removed religious control of schools and established a secular system instead. The Catholic bishops, like the various Protestant denominations, were alarmed. As one commentator pointed out: 'If the bishops had to choose between accepting the northern state and losing their schools, then they were going to keep their schools.'[23] By the time the next election was held, in 1925, the nationalist politicians had responded to pressure from the Church, Catholic business interests, and the Catholic middle class in general, and agreed to take their seats if elected. 'Business, after all, had to go on'.[24]

Unlike Sinn Féin which continued to oppose the state, or indeed, the Labour representatives elected to several predominantly Catholic, working class constituencies, the Nationalist Party had close links with the Catholic clergy. Eleven of the Nationalist Party candidates in the 1925 election were proposed by priests. And a letter to the newspapers from Nationalist Party leader, Joe Devlin, announcing an end to his party's abstentionist stance, was accompanied by an open letter from Archdeacon Convery of Belfast, urging Catholics to 'unite like a bar of steel all over the six counties'.[25] The Catholic hierarchy's support for 'constitutional nationalism' remained unaltered, even within a statelet which, of its very nature, was designed to withstand any constitutional challenge from its permanent Nationalist minority.

In the 1930s the Catholic authorities throughout Europe were so obsessed with the 'evil of socialism' that they aligned themselves with the rise of fascism. Irish 'Blueshirts' were blessed by bishops as they set off to fight in the 'crusade' against the

Spanish republic, while Republicans and other radicals were subjected to strident condemnation. When the Catholics and Protestants of working class Belfast united against the state in the Outdoor Relief Strike of 1933, the Catholic hierarchy issued Lenten pastorals denouncing what they termed 'communism'.[26] Two years earlier, a more lengthy pastoral had attacked the IRA and the political organisation, Saor Éire, which was described as 'frankly communistic in its aims':

> The published programme, as reported in the press, when reduced to simple language is amongst other things, to mobilise the workers and working farmers of Ireland behind a revolutionary movement to set up a communistic state. That is: to impose upon the Catholic soil of Ireland the same materialistic regime, with its fanatical hatred of God, as now dominates Russia and threatens to dominate Spain...
>
> It is our duty to tell our people plainly that the two organisations to which we have referred, whether separate or in alliance, are sinful and irreligious and that no Catholic can lawfully be a member of them...[27]

Within two weeks of this pastoral the Dublin government had passed a law making the IRA and Saor Éire illegal. Repressive measures, once again, had been given a moral mandate by the Catholic leadership which had remained silent as the jails were filled by another generation of Republicans. The silence continued ten years later, through a period of internment north and south, and as several of the interned prisoners were executed on the orders of the Dublin government.

A renewed IRA campaign in the 1950s was denounced by Cardinal D'Alton on Christmas Eve 1955, and in January 1956 the Catholic hierarchy issued a detailed statement on war which might have been written at any period, before or since 1798, and in any colonial situation where Church leaders consistently supported the status quo, except where its own interests were directly threatened. The bishops declared:

> Catholic moral teaching lays down precise conditions in order that war be at all lawful. War is the cause of great evils, physical, moral and social. It is not lawful, unless it be declared and waged by the supreme authority of the

State. No private citizen or group or organisation of citizens has the right to bear arms or to use them against another State, its soldiers or citizens. Just as no private citizen has the right to inflict capital punishment, so he has not the right to wage war. Sacred Scripture gives the right to bear the sword and to use it against evil-doers to the supreme authority and to it alone. If individuals could arrogate to themselves the right to use military force there would be disorder and chaos, leading inevitably to tyranny and oppression.

The second condition for a lawful war is that there be a just cause. It must be certain that all peaceful means have been tried and found unavailing, that the matter at issue far outweighs the havoc that war brings and that it is reasonably certain that war will not make things worse. No private individual has authority to judge these issues, or to involve the people from whom he has received no mandate, in the serious losses inevitable in hostilities...

Acting then in virtue of the authority conferred on us by our sacred office, we declare that it is a mortal sin for a Catholic to become a member of an organisation or society which arrogates to itself the right to bear arms or to use them against its own or another State; that it is also sinful for a Catholic to co-operate with, express approval of, or otherwise assist any such organisation or society and that, if the co-operation or assistance be notable, the sin committed is mortal...[28]

This statement, which was a rejection of the centuries-long struggle for Irish liberation from British rule, is all the more remarkable when we consider that a decade later the Catholic hierarchy and clergy joined with the political establishment of the twenty-six county state in celebrating the fiftieth anniversary of the 1916 Rebellion, an armed uprising which their predecessors had vociferously denounced; Cardinal Conway presided at a memorial Mass to mark the event. But then the twenty-six county state had itself been established as a consequence of a war fought by an army of citizens against the lawful authority of the British government.

Retrospective endorsement of revolution in 1966 and in 1898 says a good deal more about the politics of the Irish Catholic hierarchy than about its theology.

As Michel Peillon wrote:

> This agility in coming to terms with those who hold the reins of power attests the political realism of the Church but at the same time betrays its conservatism, since it is seen as always trailing behind events, acting as a barrier to any social changes that might upset the status quo...It is obviously to be expected that the Church will always be favourable to the type of society which facilitates its own survival.[29]

In its hostile response to the United Irishmen, the Fenians and the revolutionaries of 1916 through the 1960s and today, the Catholic hierarchy has demonstrated opposition to any contemporary movement for radical change, where it perceives that the change might threaten its own sectional interests. When the perceived threat has passed the hierarchy will make its peace with those it once condemned, particularly if they emerge as the new establishment, as in the case of those who took power in the twenty-six counties; indeed, it may even lay claim to have been a part of the revolutionary process. Only where a revolutionary state challenges the power and social influence of the Church hierarchy and gives the people control over their own affairs, as in modern Nicaragua, will the blessings of the Church authorities be withheld from the State.

To understand this policy we must look at the historical alliance of Church and State since the early years of Christianity, and especially during the period of European colonialism in Latin America, Africa and Asia. That alliance was acceptable because of a spiritualised and individualistic approach to faith and spirituality. Unjust social and economic structures were not seen as the concern of the Church. We must also examine the break-up of this historical alliance as the oppressed peoples of Latin America and Africa challenge the European theology and colonial mentality of the Church and set about the task of building a vibrant church of the poor and oppressed.

SECTION TWO:

HISTORICAL RELATIONSHIP
BETWEEN CHURCH AND STATE

CHAPTER 4
Church and State — An Overview

*'When the Church was in the catacombs it was a Church of martyrs,
it was pure and it was prophetic. But when the Church
leaves the catacombs, when it comes down from the Cross
it easily prostitutes itself. I am referring specifically to
the Church as hierarchy, as clergy, as ecclesiastical structure.
We have to recognise that this Church is not poor.
Not even in Brazil can we say that the Church is poor.
It may be a Church of the poor only if it is poor itself.'*
(BISHOP PEDRO CASALDALIGA: *Maryknoll Magazine*, JULY 1987)

The role of the Irish Catholic hierarchy (and of the Vatican officials) in supporting the British government in Ireland, and in defending the political status quo against the people's attempts to overthrow it, is not unusual or unique as the history of the Church's role in Latin America shows quite clearly. Just as the Irish Catholic bishops have failed to confront the British government which has been responsible for a campaign of assassination and repression in Ireland, so also the Catholic hierarchies in many Latin American countries have supported the colonial and neo-colonial regimes in that region. It is estimated that 50 million Indians were slaughtered in the Spanish and Portuguese conquests in Latin America. Yet, the Catholic Church allowed itself to be aligned with these colonial governments. Although there were some notable exceptions, such as the priest Bartolomeo de las Casas, and Bishop Antonio Valdivieso who died in defence of the rights of Indians in Nicaragua, the general pattern was one of colonialism where, as theologian Enrique Dussel has stated, 'the Church made use of the State to build its churches, send out its missionaries, protect its holdings, publish its books, educate its agents. In return the State received legitimation for its subjugation of the Creoles, Indians and black slaves.'[1] Of course, the hierarchy was convinced that the best interests of the Church lay in aligning itself with the temporal powers, and the Church did, undoubtedly, achieve a degree of power and wealth it otherwise would not have gained—but at the price of becoming an accomplice to injustice and repression. The Church had come a long way from the catacombs.

The Christian Church of the early centuries was a persecuted Church— 'the Church of the Catacombs'. In a Roman Empire where the Emperor himself was a god, Christians who sought freedom of conscience and religious freedom were seen as a threat to the security of the State and were regarded as subversives. In AD 64, it was maliciously rumoured that the Christians were responsible for the burning of Nero's Rome, and many were martyred during the severe persecution which followed.

The Gospel of Christ had a radical message about wealth and the ownership of private property, and called for a radical way of life which was reflected in the way the first Christian communities lived. 'All whose faith had drawn them together held everything in common; they would sell their property and possessions and make a general distribution as the need of each required' (Acts 2:44-45). Their faith, then, had important social implications which brought them into conflict with the authorities.

Within the Christian tradition the acceptance of private property was highly qualified. The use of material goods was determined by two principles which run through all the Christian writing; firstly, the principle of self-sufficiency where everyone is to have enough of this world's goods so that he or she is self-sufficient and secondly, the principle of community which states that material goods were created for the use of all and so must be shared by all.

During this early period, the Church was active in supporting the poor against corrupt officials and landlords. Despite many obstacles the Christian communities looked after the needs of the poor effectively. Money was raised by collections during services, by special contributions in emergencies or by larger donations, all voluntary. The Church of the first three centuries, following the example of Christ, held to the view that possessions were merely a gift of God to be used for the benefit of all; wealth was to be shared with those who had nothing.

In looking after the poor, the pre-Constantinian Church had created a quasi-state organisation that looked after its members in a way that was not possible for the State. It was precisely this active help for the poor, which within the Church was seen as a major task, that created one of the organisational preconditions for the Church's incorporation in the State under Constantine. The Church had shown that it was capable of building up an efficient system under the bishops' leadership in order to provide material aid. It had also given some first indications of how it might be possible to provide a balance between social differences and contrasts. For the most part it had succeeded in uniting rich and poor without major conflicts by calling on the former to show solidarity and to use their wealth for socially-beneficial ends.[2]

That was the ideal; the reality often did not match up.

By the year AD 311, the status of Christians in the Empire had changed as a result of the Church's growing strength in society. Constantine, impressed with the Christian God, came to favour the Christian religion over the pagan religions.[3] Constantine did not see Christianity as a threat to the Empire, rather he thought it could be used as a unifying and pacifying influence. Christianity became the official religion of the Roman Empire, thus beginning an alliance with the State which has determined the Church's official social and political role to the present time.

For the most part, the exploiters and the exploited now belonged to the same Christian community, and it soon became clear that Christians were no better than non-Christians when they fell under the spell of the 'unnatural beast', wealth. Concerning the habits of some wealthy Christians, Clement of Alexandria, remarked:

> It is farcical and downright ridiculous for men to bring out urinals of silver and chamber-pots of transparent alabaster, as if grandly ushering in their advisers, and for rich women in their silliness to have privvies made of gold. It is as if the wealthy were not able to relieve nature except in a grandiose style.[4]

Some writers were critical of the attitude of the rich to the poor. John Chrysostom, who was Bishop of Constantinople about the year AD 200 observed:

> Tell me then how did you become rich? From whom did you receive that large estate and from whom did he receive it who transmitted it to you...? The root and origin of it must have been injustice. Why? Because God in the beginning did not make one man rich and another poor...He left the earth free to all alike. Why then if it is common have you so many acres of land, while your neighbour has no portion of it? Is it not an evil that you alone enjoy what is common...?[5]

Chrysostom was not too popular with the large landowners but he kept on denouncing them:

> This is robbery, not to share one's resources. Perhaps what I am saying astonishes you...not only to rob others' property but also not to share your own with others, is robbery and greediness and theft...The rich are in possession of the property of the poor, even if it is a patrimony they have received, even if they have gathered their money elsewhere.[6]

Ambrose of Milan also stressed the causes of poverty: 'Do spacious halls exalt you? They should rather sting you with remorse, because while they hold crowds they exclude the cry of the poor...'[7]

The early Christian writings were a direct challenge to the rich and powerful; John Chrysostom put the direct question: 'Did you not come naked from the womb? Will you not return naked into the earth?'[8] These words may have fallen on deaf ears but they did have the effect of raising awareness about injustice:

> One of the achievements of Christianity was to have fixed in people's consciousness the idea that it was everyone's duty to relieve the distress of one's fellow human beings. But it did not break the structures that led to impoverishment. And the claim that the poor had a right to assistance disappeared more and more. Instead they became objects of solicitude.[9]

The early Christian conviction about wealth and ownership was soon forgotten by Church officials who came to model themselves on secular princes. The Christian message had become sanitised as the Church aligned itself with the ruling classes. The Church-

State alliance was strengthened as an educated clergy became the ministers and advisers to the political rulers in return for State protection.

During the Middle Ages (AD 600-1300) the power and wealth of the Church increased. The Pope became a temporal ruler of the Papal States and formed alliances with powerful rulers in Europe like Charlemagne. On one occasion Charlemagne wrote to the Pope that it was the Pope's job to pray for the Church, and his job as emperor, to rule it.[10] Bishops were appointed by the emperor or king, and the Church was modelled on the monarchy with the Pope at the head wearing a crown. In the later Middle Ages as the power and wealth of the Church increased so did the abuses, as clergy from the Pope down became more worldly and materialistic.

There had always been some within the Church who protested at the materialistic and worldly direction of the Church as an institution. Initially the monastic orders had tried to separate the Church from worldly power and call it back to its original simplicity and purpose, that of defending the poor and acting in solidarity with the oppressed. Francis of Assisi (1181-1226) had tried to witness to a different set of values.

Two strands run through the history of the Church down to our own day. The one, the Constantinian tradition, emphasises sin in order to legitimise the State and its rulers as willed by God because the people are not capable of freedom and self-determination. The other, the apocalyptic or prophetic tradition, holds that the Son of Man had defeated sin and, therefore, the power of the people to create a new society has to be released. The Constantinian model has sanctioned all kinds of class domination from slavery to serfdom to wage labour, and has placed the Church in collaboration with the different ruling classes.[11] It was this Church-State alliance which led to the Inquisitions (1233-1300) when 'heretics', those who challenged the status quo, were burned at the stake. And a new dimension was brought to the 'Church Militant' by the crusades and the Church's military orders, when the Church became a temporal political organisation in the name of religion.

When the hierarchy failed to deal with the Church's alliance with the rich, one of the most serious crises in the Church's history occurred. The rebellion of the Augustinian priest, Martin Luther, and the Reformation (1517-1650) prompted others to set about internal reforms. The meeting of the Pope and bishops at the Council of Trent (1545-63) placed great emphasis on the authority of the Pope and the need for obedience. Official theology after Trent put renewed emphasis on unquestioning obedience to authority. The people were instructed to obey not just their spiritual leaders but their temporal leaders as well, since they too received their authority from God. Those at the bottom of the heap who had to endure a life of poverty were promised a better time in the 'next world'. With the rise and development of capitalism, the Church became a mainstay of the master/slave system and did not question the policies of the Catholic colonial rulers.

As a consequence of this political alliance of Church and State, the Christian religion came to play the role of legitimising, and even making sacred, the social and economic structures of colonial governments. It also served as propagandist to cover up and justify existing conditions of repression and poverty. 'God in his heaven, the King on his throne, the landlord on his estate—that was the order of things, God's eternal and sacred order.'[12]

The doctrine of the 'divine right of kings' came to be accepted in the Catholic countries of Europe after the Protestant Reformation and the Wars of Religion (1618-48). During this period France took over from Spain as the leading power in Europe, and throughout most of this century France was governed in effect by two Catholic Cardinals, Richelieu (died 1642) and Mazarin (died 1661), on behalf of the Sun King, Louis XIV.

With the French Revolution (1789-94), the Catholic Church's alliance with the rich and powerful was once again underlined. The revolutionary movement, which abolished the monarchy of Louis XVI and set up a revolutionary government, threatened the Church's power and authority, and was vehemently opposed. Thousands of Catholics were killed; many were forced to flee the country. Pope Pius VI, taken prisoner to France, died there in 1799, some revolutionaries claiming that the last Pope had died. However, relations between France and the new Pope, Pius VII, improved with the coming to power of Napoleon Bonaparte, though the Pope refused to support Napoleon's war against Britain.

In 1818, when the movement for independence was sweeping across Latin America, the Pope wrote to the bishops there: '...as one of the best precepts of our religion is that which enjoins submission to superior authorities, we do not doubt that in the riots that are taking place in those countries...you will not have ceased to inspire your flocks with the firm and righteous hatred which they must feel towards them.'[13] In another encyclical in 1847 the Pope refers to the independence movements as 'the thistle sown by the enemy'.[14] Such papal pronouncements did nothing to halt the movements for political freedom from the colonial rulers that were gaining momentum in the nineteenth century.

In 1775 two-thirds of the world population lived under colonial domination; in 1945 the population of the colonies still represented 45% of the world's population.[15] But by 1970 the percentage had dropped to 3%. Even the organisers of the United Nations had not foreseen such a rapid development. In 1945 fifty-one states assembled to found the United Nations. The headquarters, then under construction in New York, was planned 'with foresight' for 70 states; twenty years later the number of member states had risen to 114, most of the new members coming from the Africa-Asia block and by 1972 the total had reached 136.

These political developments in the twentieth century have forced the Catholic Church to come to terms with rapidly-changing circumstances, not the least of which are the oppressed people's struggles to end the colonial rule with which the Catholic Church had become so closely identified. Dom Helder Camara recalls a time when the Latin American bishops thought it was their duty as shepherds 'to help maintain the existing social order', and he says, 'it seemed normal that Christ's Church was helping to maintain the governments and the rich in power.'[16] A realisation that two-thirds of the world lived in poverty caused the bishops to rethink in the light of Jesus' words 'I was hungry...' (Mt. 25).

A realisation also that the Catholic Church's alignment with the fascist regimes in Europe throughout the 1930s and 1940s, and in particular the Church's silence about Nazi brutality in Germany has caused many in the Church to question the Church's official attitude to the State and the Church's proper role in society. The results of that questioning are reflected in many of the documents of the Second Vatican Council.

In those instances where the Church leaders have changed their allegiance by taking sides with the poor and oppressed in their struggles for justice, the Church has suffered persecution, sometimes described as 'the return to the catacombs'.[17] Bishops, priests, catechists are condemned by the government and the media. Some have been murdered; many imprisoned. Through

Basic Christian Communities, (small grass-roots groups which meet to pray, study the Bible and organise), the poor and oppressed have discovered new hope and inspiration in their struggle for freedom and justice. Needless to say, this change has created enormous conflict and tension within the Catholic Church between those who believe in the 'theology of power and obedience' and those who believe in a prophetic theology, the Theology of Liberation. As this conflict is being worked out a new Church is being born — a Church of the Poor and Oppressed, no longer based or dependent on the European Church. This radical departure from previous social and political alignments marks the beginning of a new era — the third — in the history of the Catholic Church.

CHAPTER 5
Conflict in the Church — Two Theologies

*'The Church is, and wishes to be, the Church of all
but principally the Church of the poor.'*
(POPE JOHN XXIII)

Since the 1960s, as a result of the struggles of the poor especially in
Latin America but also in Asia and Africa, a 'reformation' has
occurred within the Catholic Church. A new Church has
emerged—the Church of the Poor; and a new theology has grown
within the Church of the Poor — the theology of liberation. This
new Church emerged against a background of fascist governments
and dictatorships which were traditionally supported by the
Catholic Church hierarchy and by the United States government.

Liberation theology has its origins then in the struggles of the
poor and oppressed to overcome their situation of oppression and
tyranny. It is a theology that is different from the traditional
Catholic theology in that it is based on experience, not on theory;
on the experience of oppressed people who are engaged in direct
action to secure justice. As one of its first proponents, Gustavo
Gutierrez, has said: 'The theology of liberation is not born from
reflection but from the reality of the poor.'[1]

The Scriptural basis for a theology of liberation can be seen in
the many references to solidarity with the poor as the real
expression of faith in the true God. Throughout the Old Testament
God is seen as the God of the Poor and the Oppressed. In the New
Testament also Christ stated that his mission was 'to bring good
news to the poor' (Luke 4), while at the same time he confronted
the wealthy, saying 'woe to you rich because you have received
your comfort' (Luke 6:24). A Church which aligns itself with or
allows itself to be used by the rich and powerful is, therefore, the
antithesis of the Church founded by Christ.

The 'official' Church, which identifies with the powerful and
preaches patience and passivity to the poor with the promise of
better things to come in the next world, is being challenged by the

emerging Church of the Poor which is identified with the oppressed and powerless — the unemployed, the exploited, the homeless, the women and children. The poor are no longer seen as the objects of history but the subjects of history in that they have taken the future into their own hands.

While this change within the Catholic Church is often identified with the Second Vatican Council it must be said that Pope John XXIII had already attempted to change the focus of the Church's social teaching even before the Second Vatican Council.[2] His encyclical, *Mater et Magistra* (1960), was the first step in the new direction and questioned the traditional theology which put stability before justice. Pope John XXIII wanted to distance the Church from alignments with ultra-conservative groups and governments. The Second Vatican Council followed Pope John's approach to social teaching. The Council had developed the notion of social justice as fundamental to the achievement of peace.[3]

The Second Vatican Council had a major influence on future developments, especially in Latin America. In its document 'The Church in the World' (*Gaudium et Spes*) the Council had put forward a new model of Church-State relations, a model in which the Church would be free to condemn social injustice. Above all, the Second Vatican Council opened the way for a radical approach to the issue of injustice and inequality in the Third World, an approach that was clearly outlined by the Conference of Latin American Bishops, meeting at Medellin, Colombia, in 1968 to apply the ideas of the Second Vatican Council to their particular situation.[4]

The Medellin Conference in 1968 was a turning point in the Latin American Church. Throughout Latin America, bishops, priests and religious made an option for the poor which meant a radical change of life-style. As a result of this option they refused to get involved in condemnations of any aspect of the people's struggle knowing that to do so is to play into the hands of the oppressor and gives the State forces justification for further repression.[5] Rather than condemning the activities of the oppressed, they focus on the unjust structures, the unjust institutions and laws which provoke rebellion in the first place. In trying to end political violence, liberation theology addresses the causes — not the symptoms — of violence.

This interpretation of the Christian faith conflicts quite sharply with the Constantinian interpretation associated with the European Church, a Church still infected with the colonial mentality and its emphasis on obedience, acceptance of the status quo and on the concept of individual sin. This individualistic religion does not recognise that social and economic structures can be sinful, nor that it is the Christian's duty to work to abolish unjust structures.

From the perspective of the Church of the Poor, a religion which is confined to preaching and moralising is a mockery of Christianity; a religion which is about 'saving the soul' while allowing the body to be brutalised is a complete distortion of the Gospel. Liberation theology protests against other-worldliness which ignores the reality of poverty and oppression. The God of the Bible has a special love for the poor and oppressed not because God does not love everybody, but because poverty and oppression represent the breakdown of God's overall intention for human existence.[6]

In 1985 a group of concerned Christian activists in South Africa issued the Kairos document — *A Challenge to the Church* — presenting the alternative to the official Church theology.[7] Their statement challenges both 'state theology' and 'Church theology' and argues that the mistakes and misunderstandings of the Church in the South African situation can be attributed to the type of faith and spirituality that has dominated the Church. It has been other-worldly, purely private and individualistic, relying on God to intervene to put right what is wrong. From this viewpoint, there is little anybody can do other than be patient and pray for God to intervene.

According to the Kairos statement, the present crisis in South Africa calls for a radical response from the Church which involves 'reading the signs of the times' (Mt.16:13) or 'interpreting the Kairos' (Lk.12:56) or, more simply, social analysis. The first fact in an analysis of the South African situation is that it is not a racial conflict. It is a situation of oppression and the conflict is a *moral* one between an oppressor and the oppressed — two irreconcilable viewpoints, one of which is just, the other unjust. No compromise is possible. According to those involved in the struggle, it is the apartheid system itself which is the basic evil and which must be removed.

The statements of the Church leaders in relation to the conflict are often regarded by Church members, active in the struggle, as both superficial and counter-productive because, instead of basing such statements on an analysis of the situation, they merely 'repeat a few stock ideas derived from Christian tradition without any explanation of what they imply.'[8] Traditional theological concepts, such as the 'need for reconciliation' are misplaced, Kairos argues, since reconciliation is not the key to the resolution of conflicts between what is just and what is inherently unjust, between good and evil:[9]

> To speak of reconciling these two is not only a mistaken application of the Christian idea of reconciliation but is a total betrayal of all the Christian faith has ever meant. Nowhere in the Bible or in tradition is it ever suggested to reconcile God and the Devil. We are called to do away with evil, injustice, oppression and sin — not to come to terms with it. We are supposed to oppose, confront and reject the devil — not to sup with him. It would be unChristian to plead for reconciliation before the present injustices have been removed. To plead reconciliation is to play into the hands of the oppressor, to become silent accomplices, to become 'servants of the devil'. We must preach repentance not reconciliation to those who support injustice.

The Kairos also questions the Church's concept of the term 'justice' and concludes that often what is meant is not justice but reformism, a relaxation in the symptoms of oppression which is determined by the oppressor and offered, begrudgingly, to the people as a concession that is intended to keep them quiet. The Kairos points out that the measure of what constitutes justice must be determined by the oppressed, not the oppressor.[10]

Similarly, in terms of the Church's view on 'violence', the Kairos states that in situations of conflict between the oppressed and the State, the statements of religious leaders blame the people and fail to recognise the existence of institutional violence. The Church leaders say that they condemn all violence, but is it legitimate to use the same word 'violence' in a blanket condemnation to cover the ruthless and repressive activities of the State and the desperate attempts of the people to defend themselves?[11]

The authors of the Kairos document have followed the path of liberation theology which has been paved since the Second Vatican Council by the Basic Christian Communities in Latin America. These have challenged the conscience of believers throughout the world but have yet to make any real impact on the Church here in Ireland. The Basic Christian Communities are 'essentially pastoral, not political, in direction, but they do have the potential for long-term political impact'[12] because they ask basic questions as to why things are the way they are. The communities did not emerge spontaneously but were the result of an initiative of priests and religious working among the poor. The implications for the Church in Latin America have been enormous:

> Today the Latin American Church stands in the vanguard of Christianity's long, often confused, search for social justice; in some areas, such as theology and community action, it has clearly taken a leadership role. Perhaps the most interesting aspect of the Latin American Church's contribution to universal Catholicism is that it has shown that change can occur even in the most reactionary institutions, and at breathtaking speed. If two decades ago someone predicted that there would be a Church of Martyrs in Latin America, the suggestion would have been treated with total disbelief...
>
> For centuries the Catholic Church had identified with the white European conquerors, its role being to indoctrinate the Indian, Black and half-cast masses that it was God's will that they should be poor. In return the Church was given a monopoly over education and Catholicism was made the State religion in most countries. The Church also became extraordinarily rich; at one time it was the largest landowner in Latin America. Even as late as the 1950s most bishops and priests maintained a narrow, often self-serving, view of their societies, disclaiming any involvement with the poor beyond traditional charitable works...
>
> There were always exceptions, particularly in Chile and Brazil; one of the first martyrs of the Latin American Church was Nicaragua's Bishop Antonio Valdivieso, killed in the sixteenth century by Spanish settlers because of his defence of the Indians. But by and large the Latin American Church lived up to its reputation as a bigoted, theo-logically-remote and politically-reactionary institution... For all the current fuss about politics in the Latin American Church, history shows that it was always involved in politics—only they were the politics of the rich instead of the poor.[13]

The brutal murder of Archbishop Romero in El Salvador in 1980,[14] has drawn the world's attention to the new 'Church of Martyrs' in Central and South America, a Church in which more than 1,200 bishops, priests and nuns have been threatened, arrested, tortured, expelled or murdered because they have opted for the poor. Apart from direct repression, military regimes have tried to undermine the Church by encouraging the growth of conservative religious sects or the charismatic movement with its greater emphasis on individualism and personal piety in contrast to the activism and solidarity of the Christian Base Communities.[15] Fundamentalist sects which are active in the region receive substantial funding from the United States government, particularly since the Rockefeller Report of 1969 which stated that the Catholic Church in Latin America would be one of the major forces against the dictators, and ultimately American policy in the region.[16]

Cardinal Paulo Evaristo Arns, the Archbishop of Sao Paulo, Brazil, has explained why so many governments view the pastoral work of priests and religious in the Basic Communities as dangerous:[17]

> The option for the poor touches the very heart of the social system and invites the anger of all those who have benefited from an unjust economy. The poor are exploited in all aspects of this system, from the little fisherman who sells his shrimp for two cents a pound, to the factory worker in a multinational industry. The Indian loses his land and the small landowner loses his livelihood or his very life. The defence of the poor is a threat to the whole system which reacts with all the virulence of its being. Those who are not part of the system are called subversive, communists, political opportunists...
>
> Our politicians and the owners of our newspapers have become 'theologians' and are constantly preaching sermons to the Church—for our own good, of course...! They want us to bless their banks and their factories, to approve their unjust wage laws, to celebrate the days when they were victorious over the poor. And mind you, none of this would be political, it would be neutral; it would mean recognising reality—the rich and the powerful have conquered and all should rejoice...!
>
> The option for the poor is not a class option in the Marxist sense of the word. The Gospel is indeed universal, but the

powerful will only see the newness of the word of God through the eyes of the poor and through the rejection of profit as the centre and only absolute of social organisation.

Apart from State repression and the loss of its monopoly over education, the Latin American Church has also had to contend with internal division. Indeed, the Latin American Bishops' Conference, which organised the Medellin conference and a later meeting at Puebla in 1979, is now openly divided. A new conservative leadership has meant the virtual withdrawal of the Brazilian bishops, while other progressive members of the hierarchy in Latin America have also distanced themselves from the leadership.

Pressure has also come from the Vatican. In May 1984 Cardinal Ratzinger, head of the Congregation for the Doctrine of the Faith, sent a set of critical observations on the work of liberation theologian, Gustavo Gutierrez, to the bishops of Peru. When the bishops did not condemn liberation theology, as the Cardinal had hoped, he issued a second negative statement the following September.[18] In May 1985 Ratzinger summoned Leonardo Boff, prominent Brazilian theologian, to Rome and ordered him to observe a year's 'penitential silence'. Shocked by this action, many Brazilians intervened on behalf of Boff, and as a result, he was released from his sentence before the year was over. A less hurtful statement on liberation theology was released in March 1986,[19] and a month later Pope John Paul II sent a letter to the Brazilian bishops acknowledging that liberation theology 'is not merely opportune; it is useful and necessary'.

Believing that the theology of liberation does not originate with them but with the poor, liberation theologians have been relatively unworried by the debate with the Vatican. Mexican theologian, Raul Vidales, explains:[20]

> If they want to kill off the theology of liberation—we said to the most important Church dignitaries—then finish off the poor. You can condemn the theologians but this is not the problem. The problem is that the poor have appropriated the Gospel of Jesus Christ, expropriating what has been held captive by the wealthy classes, including the high ecclesiastical dignitaries...The full theology of liberation is when the people express, verbalise their living of the faith, their celebration of the joy in the

Gospel, with their own words, with their own cultural expression, with their own way of communicating.

Vidales rejects the theory that the theology of liberation has come to divide the Church, but emphasises that the Church 'does not lie outside a society divided into social sectors' and that 'the only thing liberation theologians come to do is to take sides with one of the sectors — the poor'.[21] As to the notion that there are two Churches, Vidales is adamant:

> There is only one Church. This is something very important to underline, because the more comfortable way for the institutional Church would be for the Basic Communities to declare themselves outside the Church. We are the one Church of Jesus Christ. I believe that in the polemic with the Vatican over the theology of liberation, this has been the big problem. This term 'Popular Church' has been manipulated to mean a different Church, standing against the hierarchy. No! We are all the one Church...[22]

Vidales also stresses that this Church 'sprouting from the people is evangelising its pastors, contrary to what occurred before, when the people were the ones who were evangelised. Now the people evangelise.'[23]

Such a reversal of roles would be a radical departure in Ireland in a Church which has been traditionally so identified with the hierarchy and so dominated by the clergy. The initiative needs to come from the priests and religious who are prepared to put social justice before social control and who are willing to work alongside the poor and oppressed in their struggles even if it means being misunderstood and castigated.

Liberation theology, which affirms the people's right to resist injustice and oppression, has sometimes been mistakenly associated with the use of military means as if traditional theology was pacifist. While liberation theology allows for the Catholic Church's teaching on the justified revolution it calls on those with power in the Church to show the oppressed how an unjust tyranny can be ended by peaceful non-violent means.

CHAPTER 6

The Catholic Church and Revolution

'There never was a pacifist Christian Church.
There were Christian pacifists but the Christians as a body never,
even from the beginning, had a pacifist theology.'
(DES WILSON, *An End To Silence*)

One of the most important developments within the liberation theology debate is a deeper understanding of the meaning of violence. There is no attempt to glorify violence in any way but to understand and define violence and, above all, to underline and confront the causes of violent conflict. As with liberation theology in general this new understanding of violence has developed from the perspective of the poor and oppressed.[1]

The Catholic Church is not, nor has it ever been, a pacifist Church. There have been Christian pacifists but Christians even in the early days did not have a theology of non-violence; in fact leaders of the Church have blessed armies, weapons and war as part of their alliance with government. Bishops and even saints have served as soldiers as well as ministers of religion; 'Holy Crusades' against the infidel secured indulgences for a warrior class in the middle ages as did participation in the religious wars centuries later. In recent times moral sanction was given to opposing sides in the two world wars and to the armed forces of governments throughout the world — all in clear contradiction to the words of Christ about having any truck with secular powers and 'principalities'.

The Church's teaching on the Just War developed in its early stages as a form of defence for the poor in a Europe ravaged by war during the so-called Dark Ages.[2] This theory, however, evolved as a justification for state violence and denunciation of popular insurrection against the status quo. It is on the basis of this distorted theory of the 'Just War' that the Catholic Hierarchy has argued that the established authority must be upheld and obeyed and to wage war on that authority is morally indefensible.

There is, however, another traditional theory in Catholic theology which does in fact uphold the rights of citizens in certain circumstances to wage war against a tyranny.[3] The problem is that Church leaders have become so aligned with governments that they will seldom, if ever, acknowledge the moral legitimacy of a people's revolution — certainly while it is in progress. It is only when it is successful that the hierarchy is prepared to change sides. The Irish bishops condemned the 1916 Rebellion but later endorsed it and commemorated the leaders. The Irish bishops in common with bishops in many other countries supported the 1956 revolution in Hungary against the government — a government which did not have the interests of the Church at heart.

The Church's theology of the Just Revolution was reaffirmed by Pope Paul VI[4] and by the recent Vatican document *Instruction on Christian Freedom and Liberation* (1986)[5] which stated: '...where there is recourse to armed struggle, which the Church's Magisterium admits as a last resort, to put an end to an obvious and prolonged tyranny which is gravely damaging the fundamental rights of individuals and the common good.' The Church's theology of the Just Revolution was clearly on the side of the oppressed and allowed for the taking up of arms to get rid of an unjust and intolerable tyranny. The problem is that there has never been any discussion about this within the Irish Church.

For its part, liberation theology differentiates between three distinct forms of violence.[6] First, there is institutional or dominant violence, the violence of the State in denying social, political or economic justice either to its own people or to a subject people. The second type of violence is the repressive violence of the State embodied in the laws of the State and in the structures of social control and used to defend the state; these together constitute the primary violence in situations of conflict between the State and the oppressed. The third kind of violence is the violence used by the oppressed attempting to confront and overcome the primary violence of the state.

Liberation theology holds that these forms of violence are not equal, that the primary violence is that of the State itself which is morally indefensible while the violence of the oppressed may be justified where non-violent means are denied or are rendered ineffective by the State — the Oppressor.

Given that the institutional or State violence is the greater evil since it is the source of the conflict, it follows logically that the correct moral position is to confront this violence first rather than the secondary violence of the people. Church leaders have also the further moral responsibility to refrain from condemnations of the secondary violence which will in turn be used by the State to increase repression. This does not mean that the Church leaders should not be free to make criticisms — either of the armed struggle in general or of the particular tactics, but only that it should be conscious of how such criticism might be made without providing the State with another stick to beat the people and giving them also some kind of moral approval. Above all the Catholic Church leaders have a moral responsibility, where they oppose what is called the revolutionary violence of the oppressed, to provide a viable and effective alternative which will secure justice.

As a result of this analysis of violence we can get beyond the slogans and the jargon — 'all violence is wrong' and 'murder is murder' — to a discussion about the different kinds of violence. The slogans are seen as dishonest propaganda used by those in power to divert attention from the truth about the causes of political violence and disorder.

To argue, as the Irish Catholic bishops have done, that the issue for Catholics is quite simply whether or not they support violence is a complete misrepresentation of the problem. Violence is never a morally desirable value and nobody believes it is the best way. But in particular situations of oppression it may be the only way open to people to defend themselves against injustice. Dietrich Bonhoeffer, the Protestant theologian who was himself a victim of violence under Nazi rule in Germany said: 'All that is Christian in me protests against violence and yet, in the present circumstances, I can do no other.'

The division within the Catholic Church then is not really about the use of military means or armed struggle for political purposes but is a result of the age-old conflict about the rights of oppressed peoples to challenge the established government — by whatever means. The real conflict is ideological or political between those who are well-off and believe in one particular kind of society — authoritarian, hierarchical — and those who believe in another very different kind of society which is revolutionary and egalitarian.

There is no other way to understand why some Irish bishops, who praise Republican revolutionaries when they are safely dead, are so implacably opposed to Republicans who are living and are so prepared to align themselves with the British government. There is no other way to understand how any bishop in whose diocese most of his people are Republicans can allow himself to be used for British propaganda purposes.

How has the Irish Catholic Church arrived at this position which is already threatening to alienate a large section of the Catholic people — especially the poor — from the Church? The answer lies in the historical process whereby the Catholic hierarchy and senior clergy in Ireland, as elsewhere, have clearly aligned themselves with the interests of the monied and property-owning class. Given this social alignment it is not surprising that the bishops reflect the political allegiances of this class. It is also apparent that because of this social alignment members of the Catholic hierarchy seem to find more in common with their counterparts in the Protestant Churches, who are avowedly pro-British than they do with the poor and oppressed in their own congregation.

The Irish Catholic bishops, because of their traditional allegiance to the State, continue to support the State's propaganda line on 'violence' referring to 'the violence of the last twenty years' as if what existed before that was not violence. When the Irish bishops issued a Pastoral in November 1987 condemning violence as 'sinful' they left nobody in any doubt that they were referring specifically to Republican violence. There was no mention of the violence of the government's economic and military policies and the misery they were causing to the poor section of the community. As Pope John Paul II stated during his visit to Ireland in 1979:[7]

> As long as injustices exist in any of the areas that touch upon the dignity of the human person, be it in the political, social or economic field, be it in the cultural or religious sphere, true peace will not exist. The causes of inequalities must be identified through a courageous and objective evaluation, and they must be eliminated so that every person can develop and grow in the full measure of his or her humanity.

Some will say that the Irish bishops condemn all violence equally. This is not true. The Irish Catholic bishops have never confronted the violence of partition and the British interference in Ireland. Nor have they confronted the repressive violence of the State.

While individual bishops have, on occasions, protested about specific injustices, they have reserved their strongest condemnations for Republicans who believe they have no option but to use armed struggle to end the oppression.

The conflicting views about the use of armed struggle to bring about social justice is not confined to Ireland (nor indeed to the Catholic Church as was seen at the 1988 Lambeth conference when the motion on the right of oppressed peoples to use armed struggle was passed). The experience in Brazil indicates that a change of policy by the hierarchy is possible.

If the Catholic hierarchy in Ireland were to change its policy and take up the cause of the oppressed Nationalists in the north of Ireland they would define violence differently. They would understand the institutional violence 'that finds expression in the structure and daily functioning of a socio-economic and political system which accepts it as normal and usual that progress is impossible unless the majority of the people are used as a productive force under the management of a privileged minority.'[8]

The traditional attitude of the Church leadership in South Africa, has, as the Kairos Document states,[9] led to a situation where in conflicts between the oppressed and the State, the statements of religious leaders blame the people and fail to acknowledge the existence of institutional violence. It is inevitably the oppressed that are told to 'lay down their arms', not the forces of State repression. The effect of Church statements, far from curbing violence, is actually a contributing factor to violence since they are used to justify further state repression.

What is the British government doing in Ireland? Is it there to keep the peace and prevent a 'blood-bath' as their propaganda so often says? Or is it there to stop a revolution by pursuing a policy of containment — for the same reason that the American government is involved in Central America? Is the British government in Ireland for the good of the Irish people or for its own good? We need answers to these questions if we are to determine who is the aggressor and who are the oppressed. The Irish Catholic bishops must make clear their attitude to the British interference in Ireland if their moral statements about violence are to have much credibility in future.

SECTION THREE:
CONTEMPORARY SITUATION

CHAPTER 7

The People's Analysis

*'If a desire for peace leads us to abhor violence of every kind,
concern for truth must lead us to accurately state Christian teaching,
and love of justice must make us untiring in our search
for a final solution to the problem of
injustice and violence in Northern Ireland.'*
(STATEMENT BY 60 NORTHERN PRIESTS, JANUARY 1972)

It is the structural injustice of partition and British interference which prevents peace in Ireland. Successive British governments have denied self-determination to the Irish people, using the tactic of 'divide and rule'. The British government has maintained control by giving marginal privileges to a selected minority of the Irish nation. In return, that minority is expected to guarantee stability for British rule by acting as a bulwark against any movement for change.

In Ireland, as in many of its other colonies, the British government used religion as the basis for dividing the people, so that a Protestant minority was given marginal advantages over the majority who are overwhelmingly Catholic. It is important to remember, however, that religion is merely the instrument of division, not its source. If, as seems possible, the British should decide that a class alliance would better suit their purpose as a vehicle for effective social control, then working class Protestants will be sacrificed. This would depend on how effectively middle class Catholics could be persuaded to act as allies and agents of British rule.

Whenever its privileged Protestant garrison has proved incapable of guaranteeing stability, we have had direct British military and political intervention to defend their strategic interests in Ireland. Twice in this century the Westminster government has responded to Republican pressure by implementing major political initiatives. The first occasion was the partition of Ireland; the second, in 1972, was the introduction of direct rule.

Partition was introduced at the height of the Anglo-Irish War (1919-21) in response to the revolutionary threat posed to British interests by the IRA campaign of that period. Unable to maintain direct control over all of Ireland, the Westminster government devised a settlement, allowing them direct control over that part of Ireland where Protestants (mainly pro-Unionist) constituted a majority, and indirect control over the remainder of Ireland which, being denied full sovereignty, would remain dependent and weakened.

An unnatural boundary was created and the Northern Ireland statelet was formed. The artificial majority set about building a Protestant state for a Protestant people, a state built on discrimination and bigotry; above all, a state created and maintained by successive British governments. When the Catholics asked Britain for justice they were informed that Britain could not interfere; however when it appeared that the state was about to be brought to its knees, the British did interfere by sending in more troops to bolster their political creation.

The colonial nature of the conflict has been underlined since the arrival of 20,000 British troops in August 1969, and in particular, since the suspension of the Northern Ireland parliament at Stormont in 1972 which introduced direct rule from Westminster. The real power brokers in the situation have always been those who hold the reins of power at Westminster. It is they who perpetuate division and conflict in Ireland, frustrating the inalienable right of the Irish nation to unity and self-determination.

The colonial reality of the northern statelet, apparent from the obvious military presence in Catholic areas, is confirmed in a 1986 report titled *A Life of Poverty — Northern Ireland*.[1] This report reveals that in some Nationalist areas the unemployment rate is more than 80%. A large section of the Catholic population has always been unemployed because of structural discrimination in employment practices, while those who did find employment in the major industries found themselves the targets of threats and intimidation from a Loyalist workforce anxious to maintain its privileged status in the skilled jobs sector.

The study found that the six counties is the most poverty-stricken and deprived area of the United Kingdom. It estimated that in 1985 at least one in three children was being raised in poverty. Indeed, the six counties ranked highest in infant mortality, housing unfitness rate and unemployment. At the same time, the northern statelet ranked lowest in amount of consumer durables, economic activity rates and proportion of job vacancies. 'Acute unemployment, low wages, a high cost of living, one-parent families and a variety of housing problems are all factors which contribute to the severe poverty found in N. Ireland.'[2] In addition, the study noted that the six counties 'suffers disproportionately from external control of companies; 78% of the manufacturing industry is controlled externally.'[3]

The study also dispelled the myth that employees' 'wage increases prevent their employers from investing enough money to stimulate the economy.'[4] Over £6 billion sterling was invested overseas in 1983 and overseas investments continue to increase under the present government. The proportion of low-paid manual workers has risen from one in eight to one in five over the past five years. On the other hand, the pay and dividends of directors of four companies, most of which operate in the north of Ireland, range between £251,000 and £778,000 sterling annually.

In 1986-87 public funding provided a budget of £3.3 million to promote the arts in Northern Ireland while only £0.3 million was provided for eradicating job discrimination.[5] More importantly, it is estimated that over the next three years £5.7 billion will be spent on security in the six counties, while spending on housing will be drastically reduced.[6]

It is the structural injustice of the Northern Ireland State which relegates people to second-class citizenship. It is the structural violence of the State which denies men and women full participation in society; it condemns children to grow up in poverty. It is the structural violence of partition which denies the Irish people their fundamental and inalienable right to national self-determination, leaving them a divided nation in a permanent state of dependency. The source of this structural violence is Britain's continued colonial interference in the affairs of the Irish people.

The Northern Establishment's violent reaction to a peaceful mass movement for civil rights brought about the recent phase of armed resistance to British rule. Based on discrimination and repression, the state could not cope with even minimal reform without reactionary convulsions. It was in the context of this structured intransigence that Republican militancy re-emerged and gained mass support.

Although it is impossible to quantify with any certainty the extent of public support for Republican militancy, the fact that the British have been unable to restore stability after 20 years proves that a sizeable section of Nationalist community must lend at least passive support to the struggle. The election results of recent years demonstrate that 40% of the Nationalist community openly supports Sinn Féin, the political wing of the revolutionary movement, despite intense pressure from their religious leaders and the media to do otherwise. It is also clear that support for the Republican position is strongest within the urban and rural working class and small farmers, the most oppressed section of the Nationalist community.

While Republican militants have not yet achieved their central objective — to compel the British to withdraw — they have forced minimal concessions and reforms from the British. As a direct result of the instability generated by the Civil Rights movement and sustained by the revolutionary struggle of the past 20 years, the British were compelled to concede demands on housing, voting rights, the suspension of Stormont, and more recently, in the area of discrimination in employment — none of which would have been achieved had it not been for popular resistance. Nor would we have had the Sunningdale Agreement, devolved government, or the Hillsborough Agreement, all of which demonstrate the British search for stability and which ultimately narrow the options facing the Westminster government until only the option of withdrawal remains.

Although many have been killed in the conflict over the past 20 years, the early deaths and bombings were caused by the British and their Loyalist allies, not by the Republican forces.[7] However, each death from whatever quarter is a result of the unresolved political problem of British colonialism, and so long as that problem remains there will be no peace. Even if the Republican forces were to end their resistance, the basic injustice will continue to fester until it is challenged by a future generation.

The British have dispensed with the 'normal' process of law and have used 'special powers' of arrest, detention, internment and remand procedures, in an effort to restore stability. They have used extra-legal methods, termed 'shoot to kill' operations, to eliminate political opponents; employed special weaponry, such as plastic bullets, to crush civil disturbances; set up special 'Diplock' courts to streamline convictions; and enacted special legislation to deny people the right to vote for the candidate of their choice.

This repressive infrastructure is backed up by tens of thousands of heavily-armed British soldiers and members of the Royal Ulster Constabulary who saturate Nationalist areas, conduct extensive house raids, seize buildings and land, and who constantly abuse and harass the local population. In working class areas every Nationalist is considered suspect by the British army; they in turn, are regarded as an army of occupation even by those who do not support the Republican armed struggle.

The British have a powerful ally in the mass media, much of which is London-based. International wire services dutifully relay the British propaganda line on events, while the domestic news services in Britain and Ireland are stifled by censorship. The thrust of the British government-sponsored media line is that the conflict is between Catholic and Protestant, that it is intractable, and that the British are there as neutral peacekeepers. Republicans are portrayed as criminal zealots, or simply as 'terrorists'. There is no attempt at genuine analysis and the views of the oppressed Nationalists are seldom if ever heard.

Despite the increasing repression and the terrible suffering of the past 20 years, the struggle for radical social and political change continues on many fronts — because of the belief that it must continue if a just and peaceful settlement is ever to be achieved. But the people are also demanding that the Catholic Church's leaders adopt a new strategy which would mean them making an option for the poor and oppressed.

CHAPTER 8

The Hierarchy's Mistaken Analysis

*'While we recognise that the authorities can make mistakes
or be guilty of abuses, we recommend that the Churches jointly
remind their members that they have a* prima facie *moral obligation
to support the currently constituted authorities in Ireland
against all paramilitary powers...'*
(VIOLENCE — A REPORT TO THE CHURCHES)

Once it had secured control over the education of Catholic children, the leadership of the Catholic Church settled down to accept the contrived Northern Ireland statelet, though hardly with any great enthusiasm. So long as it retained the substantial power which it had come to enjoy within its own 'community', the Catholic hierarchy was prepared to urge acceptance of the status quo, irrespective of the institutional discrimination suffered by the Catholic population in general.

Apart from its open condemnation of those who attempted to overthrow the State, the Catholic hierarchy were conspicuous by their absence and by their silence during the campaign of the Civil Rights Association in the late 1960s. Indeed, the paramount concern of Church leaders in that period was to curtail the development of radicalism within the Catholic population. In 1970, the then Bishop of Down and Connor, Dr Philbin, instructed Fr Des Wilson of Ballymurphy in West Belfast that Church-owned buildings were not to be made available to any members of the Civil Rights Executive. In the same year, the bishops issued a statement calling on Catholics 'to make their voices heard in repudiation of individuals or groups who may appear to be interested in the continuation of violence...',[1] and 'to co-operate with those groups who genuinely reflect the peaceful intentions of the people as a whole and who are working hard to restrain militant elements'.[2]

After 50 years of partition and of violence against Catholics, the Church authorities demonstrated by this statement that nothing had changed. In spite of all that Catholics had suffered, in spite of the pogroms and deaths during 1969, and every decade before that, their primary concern was to stifle resistance rather than to confront injustice. Furthermore, the statement manifested their continued endorsement of middle class 'constitutional' Nationalism represented by the emerging Social Democratic and Labour Party (SDLP). As in every previous generation since 1798, however, the hierarchy was quick to justify its opposition to the growing revolutionary mood on the basis that things had indeed changed.

Whereas the hierarchy, in earlier phases of the Irish revolution, based its opposition on the moral principle that the established authority must be obeyed, such an argument would have found little sympathy amongst northern Nationalists in the late 1960s and early 1970s. After all, it had been the established authority which had brutally suppressed the peaceful protests of the Civil Rights Movement. It was necessary, therefore, for the Church to shift responsibility for what had happened away from the ultimate authority, the British government, and onto the people of the six counties themselves.

However, the hierarchy's attempts to suppress the people's response to oppression did not go unchallenged. A group of 60 priests published the following statement in January 1972, a week before Bloody Sunday:

> Sweeping condemnations of the violence in Northern Ireland's minority community, and the way in which these statements have been used for propaganda by the BBC Overseas Service, force us to relate the following propositions:
>
> — it is not true to say that armed resistance to aggression can never be justified;
>
> — it is not true to say that only bishops and priests can decide when armed resistance has become lawful;
>
> — it is not true to say that only the 'elected' leaders can decide when to resist aggression and brutality with force;
>
> — the Christian tradition has always recognised the right of an oppressed community to rebel against aggression and gross injustice;
>
> — the Christian tradition has always recognised man's right to defend himself against unjust attack;

— the Christian tradition has always recognised that a rebellion which has the support of the people is lawful.

If a desire for peace leads us to abhor violence of every kind, concern for truth must lead us to accurately state Christian teaching, and love of justice must make us untiring in our search for a final solution to the problem of injustice and violence in Northern Ireland.

In search of justice we must listen especially to those who have suffered most from injustice. Those who, by position of power, are immune to the injustice of the system are not always the best informed to give guidelines to the oppressed.[3]

Having failed to recognise or to accept the colonial basis of the growing conflict in the six counties, the hierarchy inevitably portrayed the conflict as inter-communal. This analysis gave credence to the British government's propaganda that their intervention was as a peacekeeping force between Protestants and Catholics, rather than as a colonial power anxious to buttress its colony against the threat of collapse. Since colonialism had been discredited with the emergence of successful liberation movements in Africa and Asia, it was vital for Britain to convince others, internationally, that its role in Ireland was that of a peacekeeper, rather than that of a colonial power with vital strategic interests to defend.

The hierarchy has consistently refused to accept that repression and discrimination are part and parcel of a deliberate strategy or to acknowledge the British government's responsibility for the conflict. While conceding that the British have made 'mistakes', they add that those 'mistakes' either have been corrected or are in the process of being corrected. Bishop Cahal Daly, while arguing that 'some of the motives [for partitioning the country] were honourable'[4] conceded that 'it is now admitted by most observers [it] was a mistake...'[5] He also said however, 'it is unhelpful to dwell morbidly or censoriously on that past decision. It is its subsequent results and continuing effects which should solely concern us.'[6]

Bishop Cahal Daly's statement, in addition to absolving the British government from blame, conceals the centrality of partition to the conflict since it sees discrimination and repression not as a consequence of that settlement but merely as subsequent to it. Similarly, other members of the hierarchy have failed or refused to accept this point. In the wake of the early Civil Rights agitation, the northern bishops in 1970 condemned radicalism, claiming that:

> Significant changes have taken place with regard to the position of the minority in Northern Ireland during the past 18 months... As these changes—and other vitally important changes which have been promised—take effect, there will be a genuine prospect of justice and peace and further progress by orderly means.

What the bishops' statement omits is that the minimal demands which were conceded were a response to the destabilisation which the Civil Rights Movement had begun — grudging concessions aimed at defusing protest rather than creating social and political justice.

By and large the Church leadership behaves and speaks as though the British government had only a peripheral interest in events. We are told, repeatedly, that the conflict is inter-communal or tribal, and will go away when the 'two communities' each accept the other's 'traditions'. This has led, in recent years, to a perverse logic that Orangeism, and other manifestations of bigotry, should be deemed acceptable. Moreover, we are asked to admit that there are two nations in Ireland—one British, the other Irish — as opposed to one Irish nation, a section of which owes allegiance to the British government for as long as that government denies self-determination to the Irish people as a whole. This policy of appeasement towards Unionism, under the guise of ecumenism, has been demonstrated in clearly political encounters with other Church leaders and in pastoral letters in which the hierarchy has attempted to proclaim its acceptance of the State and has denounced Republicans as loudly as the British.

As in previous generations, Catholic bishops and clergy have adopted the role of a 'moral police force', attempting to control their own followers and at the same time failing to take the lead against the immorality of social and political injustice. Since the early days of the Civil Rights Movement, they have reserved their strongest condemnation for militant Nationalists and in par-ticular, for the re-emerging militancy of the IRA. This has led to revisionism, and misreading of reality, especially in the state-ments of Bishop Cahal Daly of Down and Connor, who has emerged as the chief spokesperson of the hierarchy's viewpoint. On 26 November, 1974, Bishop Daly said:

> There is no historical continuity, whatever, between the present, largely faceless, leaders of the self-styled 'Republican movement' and their honourable forebears; there is no moral continuity between their methods and those of an earlier struggle for independence. One of the aims of the present 'Republican movement' is to overthrow the very institutions of democracy which earlier Republicans sacrificed life and limb to establish.[7]

But if we recall, the contemporary Church leadership condemned those 'honourable forebears' and the reality is that at no stage did the IRA ever approve of, let alone 'sacrifice life and limb' for a partitioned Ireland. However, the British government was not worried about the inaccuracy of Bishop C.B. Daly's statement, nor that a prominent Churchman should follow the tradition of retrospective endorsement of revolution. In 1982 the bishop's statement was printed by the British Foreign and Commonwealth Office and issued for distribution in America.

In more recent times the same bishop went further into the realm of error when, during the course of a sermon delivered in Twinbrook on 24 April, 1988, he made the following accusation:

> The deterioration in the whole quality of life in West Belfast is certainly in part a consequence of the IRA's campaign. Indeed, it is not simply an indirect and unintended consequence. It is actually part of the IRA's revolutionary strategy. The ideology of revolution, which the IRA share, is that the conditions of life of an oppressed people must worsen to a point where the sufferings become unbearable, for only then will people see that nothing but total revolution will bring change and justice. If the conditions of life are not worsening of themselves, the revolutionary movement will act to make them worse and thereby hasten 'our day', the day of revolution...[8]

Social and economic deprivation breed human misery and social despair, not a revolutionary mass movement. Far from seeking to worsen the material conditions suffered by a sympathetic population, the revolution would demand that those conditions be improved, that people be given dignity and the confidence to control their own lives. This is the reality which Bishop C.B. Daly fails to recognise; instead, he has opted for an analysis which absolves the British government of its responsibility for institutionalised discrimination, poverty and repression.

And Bishop C.B. Daly is not alone. A month after the introduction of internment without trial in 1971, the six northern bishops issued a statement, which misrepresented the IRA's campaign as against the Protestants rather than against British rule and military occupation:

> In this short statement, however, we wish to focus on one fact in particular. This is, that in Northern Ireland at the present time there is a small group of people who are trying to secure a united Ireland by use of force. One has only to state this fact in all its stark simplicity to see the absurdity of the idea. Who in his sane senses wants to bomb a million Protestants into a united Ireland?[9]

So anxious were they to accommodate themselves to the political status quo that the bishops refused to condemn internment without trial. In fact, in a statement which mildly censured the torture of internees, they apologise for having to mention internment at all:

> Many Protestants in Northern Ireland—good Christian people—will not like our mentioning these things [internment]. We ask them to realise that these facts are part of the total situation... We appeal also to Catholics to realise the genuine fears and deep frustrations of the Protestant community at the present time.[10]

The British government's policy of 'Ulsterisation' which was introduced in 1976 recognised the advantage of pushing locally-recruited armed forces into the frontline in their war against the IRA because this helped to confirm the false analysis of the struggle as sectarian. The Church leadership, for its part, had already adopted this 'inter-communal' analysis, and this has had several consequences.

First, the hierarchy has been reluctant to challenge Britain's repressive policies, such as internment, on the grounds that repression is a response to social disorder. The reality is that social disorder is, in the first instance, a response to repression. Clearly, this has been the case throughout Irish history including the current conflict.

Second, as has already been stated, the overwhelming emphasis of the hierarchy has been in confronting the violence which emanates from what is termed 'the Catholic community', failing consistently to acknowledge that such violence is secondary and failing also to address themselves to the primary source of violence.

Third, we are told that the path to peace lies in reconciliation between the two divided communities. Our attitudes, rather than the political and social structures, are blamed for the division. However, attitudes are not formed in a vacuum; they are a consequence of our environment. In the context of the six counties, this means that the environment created by British rule and sustained in a sectarian statelet is the source of our attitudes and of social divisiveness.

The Church authorities fail to accept, or even to acknowledge, the direct correlation between justice and reconciliation; that without the former, the latter is impossible. For the authors of the Kairos document, this same criticism was central to understanding the basic flaw in the Church leadership's approach to the conflict in South Africa. Just as an end to the apartheid system is a prerequisite for peace and reconciliation in the South African situation, so too an end to British interference is an essential prerequisite for peace and reconciliation in Ireland. Reforms, however welcome, cannot achieve this objective if they fall short of eliminating injustice.

The calls for 'reconciliation' persist precisely because they appear reasonable. In 1978 Bishop Cahal Daly wrote that 'reconciliation between historic enemies is possible'.[11] In this he was right, but when he went on to cite the example of reconciliation between Catholics and Protestants in Holland and Germany, Bishop Daly failed to recognise that in those situations the structures which had fostered the division had been removed. On the contrary, in the context of the six counties, what is meant by 'reconciliation' is that Protestants should reconcile themselves to accepting Catholics as equals; while for Catholics, it means an acceptance of the political status quo, i.e., the Loyalist veto, and an acceptance of the institutions of the State.

The Church leadership makes no secret of the fact that it regards Republicans as the aggressors and the British as the peacekeepers. Bishop Cahal Daly co-authored an inter-Church report titled *Violence — A Report to the Churches* which read:

While we recognise that the authorities can make mistakes or be guilty of abuses we recommend that the Churches jointly remind their members that they have a *prima facie* moral obligation to support the currently-constituted authorities in Ireland against all paramilitary powers... In particular, where an individual has information about violent activities of paramilitary organisations he or she may be assuming a personal moral responsibility if... he does not put such information before the authorities.[12]

Such statements betray the pro-establishment bias of Church leaders, a bias which goes so far as to encourage people to inform to the 'authorities', a practice which has led to imprisonment and death for many. It is an unequivocal declaration of support for the British against a sizeable section of the Catholic population which rejects British rule. It is a statement which has been repeated in various forms down through the years particularly when morale is low within the Catholic Nationalist population.

* * * * *

However, the Church leadership's role as an ally of British interests goes beyond isolated pronouncements on violence. Increasingly, we find that such statements, far from being isolated, are part of a wider British counter-insurgency strategy of 'co-optation'—the recruitment of compliant elements of a subject population into an active involvement with the colonial regime. This strategy is designed to isolate Republicans within the Catholic population, while encouraging the same population to accept the institutions of British rule.

The isolation process is served by statements which denounce Sinn Féin and the IRA, while encouraging support for the SDLP; and by a policy of public confrontation which in recent years has centred on Republican funerals. Whereas there have been similar statements and confrontations in the past, today we find that these are being co-ordinated and sustained in a manner previously unknown. In 1980 when the remains of IRA man, Kevin Delaney, were refused full Catholic Church rites a decision was taken which was based on a tradition inherited from Cardinal Cullen in 1861 and Dr Cohalan of Cork in the 1920s. Today, when a priest refuses to admit a coffin, draped with the national flag, into his church, he is doing so as part of a deliberate strategy formulated in more recent times.

As if to underline the partisan nature of this strategy, the Church hierarchy still allows military funerals to members of the crown forces and has no objection to tricolour-draped coffins in the case of IRA activists of an earlier generation when these are being buried in the twenty-six counties. Through its selective policy of isolating Republican funerals, the Church authorities facilitated the introduction of a new 'get tough' strategy by the British. Funerals which would have been allowed to proceed unhindered in the past, from 1981 were subjected to persistent and brutal attacks by the RUC and British army. It was the strength of individual bereaved families in the face of such assaults, rather than any action on the part of the Church leadership, which forced the British to pull back and allow a semblance of normality to return to such occasions.

The process of encouraging Catholic acceptance of the institutions of the British state, including its armed forces, began with a series of meetings between the Northern Ireland Office (NIO) and senior figures in the Catholic middle class, including political and religious leaders, in the late 1970s and early 1980s.[13] These meetings addressed the problem of re-establishing the rule of 'law and order' into areas of Republican strength. The existence of such areas was seen as a challenge to the very fabric of social control deemed normal by both sides to the discussions. The strength of the public support for the 1980-81 hunger strikes was the first demonstrable evidence that a large section of the Catholic population was alienated not only from the institutions of the British State, but also from the social control of their own middle class leadership including the Church.

In the aftermath of the hunger strikes in 1980 and 1981 and electoral successes of Sinn Féin, the implementation of a co-optation strategy became a priority, even if that meant challenging Britain's traditional allies, the Unionists. A political process began whereby the middle class political leadership represented by the SDLP would be given a degree of power and influence. The credit for any reforms, however minimal, would be channelled to the advantage of the SDLP at the expense of Sinn Féin. This process, incorporated in the Hillsborough Agreement of 1985, was designed to undermine support for Sinn Féin, but when the first real test came in the general election of 1987, it was found to have made little difference. Apart from the paucity of reforms, the reason for the lack of results was seen to lie in the organisational weakness of the SDLP in many areas.

It is in such areas that the Church was identified as a surrogate device for political control, the means through which the revolution might be undermined. In West Belfast, the cockpit of the revolution, virtually all social and economic power is being funnelled through the Church authorities. Business empires have been established in direct opposition to independent, community-based employment schemes which are now being starved of government subsidies.

When control over employment is added to the existing control which the Catholic hierarchy exercises over the education of Catholic children, it is clear that the social power of the hierarchy has increased enormously. But it is equally clear that there has been a quid pro quo, not only in terms of isolating Republicans but also in terms of encouraging public acceptance and support for the British State and its institutions.

Apart from their statements being used by the British Information Services abroad, Catholic bishops and priests are seen in propaganda photographs in the company of British ministers. They are heard encouraging their followers to support British armed forces and they allow the schools which they control to become involved in activities organised by the RUC without the knowledge or consent of parents.

Moreover, because the social and economic power which they have gained is dependent on the British government, the Catholic hierarchy has lost whatever freedom it had in the past to confront government injustice and State violence. All of this runs contrary to the direction in which the post Second Vatican Church should be going and there is a real possibility that it will lead to more, not less, alienation, amongst those who reject British rule, from a Church which is increasingly identified as an ally of that rule.

The political bias of its spiritual leadership has gone virtually unchallenged within the Catholic Church in Ireland. The Republicans who are the victims of this bias appear to be following the age-old fashion of taking their 'politics from home, their religion from Rome'. For the rest, laity and those in religious life, there is neither enthusiasm nor criticism for the political statements which are made to appear as official Church teaching. There are exceptions on both sides, however, most notably

Republican leader Gerry Adams, who has tried and failed to discuss the Church's stance with his bishop, Dr Cahal Daly. There are anti-Republicans who use the Catholic hierarchy's statements to further their own narrow political ends. But the main beneficiary of the Catholic hierarchy's stance has been the British government which is willing to use a Catholic bishop's statement to undermine support for Irish self-determination abroad and which is prepared to allow the Catholic Church an increasing measure of social control over its adherents as part of its counter-insurgency strategy.

CHAPTER 9
Crisis or Opportunity?

'The Church's first task is "to denounce the unjust structures,
not as one who judges from without, but as one who
acknowledges her own share of the responsibility and the blame".
These brave words of Archbishop Helder Camara
refer to the whole people of God, the whole Church.
But the Church we believe in is also a hierarchical Church
with consequent distinction of roles between laity and clergy.
Although the whole Church, all Christians,
have the prophetic task of denouncing injustice,
the bishops speak with official voices. Hence,
it is not enough that laymen and priests speak out.
They also appeal to the bishops to exercise official moral leadership.'
(ED DE LA TORRE: *Touching Ground, Taking Root.*)

The present stance of the Irish Catholic Church leadership in relation to the oppression in the six counties is consistent with the stance of successive Catholic Church leaders over the past 200 years. It is a stance that is rooted in the Constantinian tradition of support for the status quo, and in the Church leadership's class alignment with the monied middle class.

Given their class alignment with the middle class, it is not surprising that Catholic Church leaders generally reflect the political allegiances and the social conservatism of this class. Nor is it surprising that they have, for the most part, a paternalistic attitude towards the working class. There appears to be an inherent bias against the working class and those who support the Republican ideal of a free and united Ireland. This bias extends to all Church-controlled employment.

The Second Vatican Council was an attempt to break out of the past, not simply in terms of liturgical and ecumenical reform but more importantly in terms of the Church's traditional alignment with political and social establishments. Henceforth, the Church leadership would attempt to reflect and represent the aspirations of 'the lower classes' which had been so contemptuously dismissed in the past: 'The joy and hope, the grief and anguish of the people of our time especially of those who are poor or afflicted in any way, are the joy and hope, the grief and anguish of the followers of Christ as well.'[1]

Apart from its moral implications, the current policy of the Irish Catholic hierarchy has resulted in a further and rapidly-growing problem—the alienation of the poor and oppressed from their Church. This has meant falling attendance at Church services, particularly amongst the young, and the undermining of episcopal authority in areas of Church teaching, apart from political pronouncements.

The teachings of the Second Vatican Council need to be applied to the oppressive situation in the north of Ireland resulting from partition — just as they have been in Latin America and elsewhere. As a first step in this process Catholic Church leaders need to adopt a different pastoral plan so as to increase the social interaction of clergy with the working class in the north. They need to listen to the oppressed and their elected representatives and what they have to say about the situation.

Moreover, they must overcome the 'we know best' attitude which has dominated such interaction in the past. This means learning the lessons of the Basic Christian Communities where the dignity and validity of working class viewpoints are accepted and applied to the way in which priests and religious deal with social, political and theological issues.

Secondly, from genuine interaction of the clergy with the poor and oppressed, the Catholic bishops will be compelled to develop a fresh analysis of the causes of political violence in our country. This analysis will go beyond a notion of peace which stops at the defeat of Republicanism to an understanding that peace and reconciliation can only be achieved by eliminating unjust structures. In the context of the age-old Irish struggle this inevitably means identifying British interference and British structures as the obstacles to peace and the guarantors of recurring conflict.

As a third step, and on the basis of this analysis, the Catholic Church working at many different levels — local, national, international — needs to develop a strategy that will lead to peace. Such a strategy will certainly involve a direct confrontation with British injustice, a confrontation that need not mean an endorsement of armed struggle, but which certainly means providing an effective alternative to such struggle. At the very least, it means an end to the condemnation of those who, in the absence of such an alternative, have felt obliged to resort to armed struggle. Such condemnations only provide the British oppressors with more propaganda and more justification for repression. It also means that the Catholic Church put justice for the oppressed Nationalists in the north of Ireland on their agenda; that they cease supporting the British government's campaign against the MacBride Principles; that the Church set up in every parish a system for recording and documenting instances of RUC brutality, harassment, torture; that the clergy take up the issue of the harassment of prisoners and the holding of prisoners as political hostages. The concern for prisoners overseas, and their families, shown by the setting up of the ICPO is a step in the right direction.

> The people look to the Church, especially in the midst of our present crisis, for moral guidance. In order to provide this the Church must first make its stand absolutely clear and never tire of explaining and dialoguing about it. It must then help people to understand their rights and their duties. There must be no misunderstanding about the moral duty of all who are oppressed to resist oppression and to struggle for liberation and justice... The Church of Jesus Christ is not called to be a bastion of caution and moderation. The Church should challenge, inspire and motivate people. It has a message of the cross that inspires us to make sacrifices for justice and liberation. It has a message of hope that challenges us to wake up and to act with hope and confidence. The Church must preach this message not only in words and sermons and statements but also through its actions, programmes, campaigns and divine services.[2]

What are the likely implications for the Catholic Church if its leaders, the bishops, break with tradition, opt for the oppressed Nationalists in the north of Ireland and enact a strategy towards achieving justice in Ireland? The same question faced the Latin American bishops when they met at Medellin (1968) and they have since had their answer: internal conflict as conservative members of the Church reacted, often violently, to the change, as well as direct State repression. It is quite likely that the Irish Church will face similar problems and that priests and bishops will have to share the harassment and outright repression which many in their congregations already face in their day-to-day lives.

On a positive note, however, the Irish Church would be stronger and would grow in respect with the Irish people especially the young for having adopted the correct moral position and for having implemented the teaching of the Second Vatican Council and of the many subsequent Church statements which refer to the task facing bishops, priests and religious in their pastoral work. Writing in 1971, Pope Paul VI called on Christians to look at 'the cause of society's ills' and 'to change unjust social and economic structures'. In the same year the World Synod of Bishops declared:

> Actions on behalf of justice and participation in the transformation of the world fully appear to us as a constitutive dimension of the preaching of the Gospel, or in other words, of the Church's mission for the redemption of the human race and its liberation from every oppressive situation.[3]

And Pope John Paul II added his voice to the need for analysis:

> As long as injustices exist in any of the areas that touch upon the dignity of the human person, be it in the political, social or economic field, be it in the cultural or religious sphere, true peace will not exist. The causes of inequalities must be identified through a courageous and objective evaluation, and they must be eliminated so that every person can develop and grow in the full measure of his or her own humanity.[4]

If there is hope today in our situation it is because of the determination of the oppressed people themselves — especially the young — to secure justice, in spite of the increasing repression. That hope always needs to be 'confirmed' and 'strengthened' as the authors of the Kairos document declared:

> At the very heart of the gospel of Jesus Christ and at the very centre of all true prophecy is a message of hope... We believe that goodness and justice and love will triumph in the end and that tyranny and oppression cannot last forever... But hope needs to be confirmed. Hope needs to be maintained and strengthened. Hope needs to be spread. The people need to have it said again and again that God is with them... There is hope. There is hope for all of us.[5]

APPENDIX 1

Rebel Priests of 1798

The following letter from Bishop James Caulfield to Archbishop Troy of Dublin (dated 2 September 1798) gives the most detailed listing of the rebel priests of 1798. It was given by Troy to Plowden, who used it in his book. The original does not now appear to be extant.

1. Thomas Dixon of Castle-bridge, had been curate at the Lady's Island for some years; but for drinking, dancing, and disorderly conduct, was suspended about four years ago. After some time of apparent amendment, he was sent to assist Rev. David Cullen of Blackwater, where he relapsed into his former pranks, and was suspected latterly of being active in the accursed business of *uniting*, for which I interdicted and suspended him above twelve months ago. He was afterwards apprehended, tried, and convicted here, and sent on board the tender lying at Duncannon Fort, where he took a fever and died.

2. Rev. Thomas Clinch, native of Camolin, had been appointed curate to Rev. Thomas Rogers in Bantry; but turning out a most beastly drunkard and unfit for duty, was suspended about two years ago, and remained so. He joined the rebels, and was killed in their retreat from Vinegar Hill.

3. Rev. Mogue Kearin or Kearns of the Duffry had been employed by Doctor Delany for some time, but latterly dismissed. He was notorious for drinking and fighting; and joined the rebels, among whom he made a gigantic figure, and was hanged at Edenderry.

4. Rev. John Murphy, curate to Rev. Patt Cogly of Boolyvogue, ever giddy, but not noted for immorality, was the first to commence the rebellion and became a signal general in it. He had been apparently but not really dutiful to his superior. He was whipped, hanged, beheaded, and his body burnt in the County Carlow, at Tullow.

5. Rev. Philip Roche, alias General Roache, had been curate to Rev. John Synnott of Gorey; had been a proper man and would be useful, but indulging in excess of drinking, and beginning to

agitate, he became obnoxious and was removed. He was afterwards sent curate, after reprehension, admonition, and instruction by his superior, to Rev. Thomas Rogers in Bantry, the other extremity of the diocese, last winter: I heard nothing remarkable of him there, till he joined the rebels and soon became a leader. He was hanged here and his body thrown into the river the 22nd June.

6. There is another reptile, Rev. Bryan Murphy, who was very active in the rebellion. He had been *deprived* and suspended about three years ago. Nevertheless he had address enough to procure a protection when the rebels were routed, and remains undisturbed.

7. There is a Rev. Mr Byrne, a Carmelite, at Goff's Bridge, who shewed himself a very zealous, active rebel. He also got a protection. He was a drinking, giddy man. I advised him to quit the diocese and threatened suspension.

8. Rev. John Keane, under censures the greater part of his life for drunkenness and other irregularities. He is a weak poor fool. He has not been questioned, nor is he worth notice.

9. Rev. John Redmond, curate of Rev. Francis Kavanagh, a most regular, attentive, zealous priest, without reproach ever until the accursed rebellion; whether he joined them through terror, as was the case with some, or volunteer'd, I know not. He surprised me more than all the rest. He was hanged near Gorey on the 21st or 22nd of June last.

Source: K. Whelan, 'The role of the priests in the 1798 Rebellion in Country Wexford'. (Kevin Whelan, *Wexford History and Society — Interdisciplinary Essays on the History of an Irish County*, Geography Publications, Dublin 1987.)

APPENDIX 2

1922 Pastoral

DEAR REV. FATHER AND BELOVED BRETHREN,

The present state of Ireland is a sorrow and a humiliation to its friends all over the world. To us, Irish bishops, because of the moral and religious issues at stake, it is a source of painful anxiety.

Our country, that but yesterday was so glorious, is now a byword before the nations for a domestic strife, as disgraceful as it is criminal and suicidal. A section of the community, refusing to acknowledge the government set up by the nation, have chosen to attack their own country as if she were a foreign power. Forgetting apparently, that a dead nation cannot be free, they have deliberately set out to make our Motherland, as far as they could, a heap of ruins.

They have wrecked Ireland from end to end, burning and destroying national property of enormous value, breaking roads, bridges, and railways; seeking by an insensate blockade, to starve the people, or bury them in social stagnation. They have caused more damage to Ireland in three months than could be laid to the charge of British rule in so many decades.

They carry on what they call a war, but which, in the absence of any legitimate authority to justify it, is morally only a system of murder and assassination of the national forces — for it must not be forgotten that killing in an unjust war is as much murder before God as if there were no war. They ambush military lorries in the crowded street, thereby killing and wounding not only soldiers of the nation, but peaceful citizens. They have, to our horror, shot bands of these troops on their way to Mass on Sunday; and set mine traps in the public roads, and blown to fragments some of the bravest Irishmen that ever lived.

Side by side with this woeful destruction of life and property there is running a campaign of plunder, raiding banks and private houses, seizing the lands and property of others, burning mansions and country houses, destroying demesnes and slaying cattle.

But even worse and sadder than this physical ruin is the general demoralisation created by this unhappy revolt — demoralisation especially of the young, whose minds are being poisoned by false principles, and their young lives utterly spoiled by early association with cruelty, robbery, falsehood and crime.

Religion itself is not spared. We observe with deepest sorrow that a certain section is engaged in a campaign against the bishops, whose pastoral office they would silence by calumny and intimidation and they have done the priesthood of Ireland, whose services and sacrifices for their country will be historic, the insult of suggesting a cabal amongst them to browbeat their bishops and revolt against their authority.

And, in spite of all this sin and crime, they claim to be good Catholics, and demand at the hands of the Church her most sacred privileges, like the Sacraments, reserved for worthy members alone. When we think of what these young men were only a few months ago, so many of them generous, kind-hearted and good, and see them now involved in this network of crime, our hearts are filled with bitterest anguish.

It is almost inconceivable how decent Irish boys could degenerate so tragically, and reconcile such a mass of criminality with their duties to God and to Ireland. The strain on our country for the last few years will account for much of it. Vanity, and perhaps self-conceit, may have blinded some who think that they, and not the nation, must dictate the national policy. Greed for land, love of loot and anarchy, have affected others, and they, we regret to say, are not a few. But the main cause of this demoralisation is to be found in false notions on social morality.

The long struggle of centuries against foreign rule and misrule has weakened respect for civil authority in the national conscience. This is a great misfortune, a great drawback, and a great peril, for a young government. For no nation can live where the civil sense of obedience to authority and law is not firmly and religiously maintained. And if Ireland is ever to realise anything but a miserable record of anarchy, all classes of her citizens must cultivate respect for and obedience to the government set up by the nation, whatever shape it takes, while acting within the law of God.

This defect is now being cruelly exploited for the ruin, as we see, of Ireland. The claim is now made that a minority are entitled, when they think it right, to take up arms and destroy the national government. Last April, foreseeing the danger, we raised our voices in the most solemn manner against this disruptive and immoral principle. We pointed out to our young men the conscientious difficulties in which it would involve them, and warned them against it. Disregard of the Divine Law, then laid down by the bishops, is the chief cause of all our present sorrows and calamities.

We now again authoritatively renew that teaching: and warn our Catholic people that they are conscientiously bound to abide by it, subject, of course, to an appeal to the Holy See.

No one is justified in rebelling against the legitimate government, whatever it is, set up by the nation and acting within its rights. The opposite doctrine is false, contrary to Christian morals, and opposed to the constant teaching of the Church. 'Let every soul,' says St Paul, 'be subject to the higher powers'; that is, to the legitimate authority of the state. From St Paul downwards, the Church has inculcated obedience to authority, as a divine duty as well as a social necessity; and has reprobated unauthorised rebellion as sinful in itself and destructive of social stability: as it manifestly is. For if one section of the community has that right, so have other sections the same right, until we end in general anarchy. No one can evade this teaching, in our present case, by asserting that the legitimate authority in Ireland just now is not the Dáil or Provisional Government. That government has been elected by the nation, and is supported by the vast majority of public opinion. There is no other government, and cannot be, outside the body of the people. A Republic without popular recognition behind it is a contradiction in terms.

Such being the Divine Law, the guerrilla warfare now being carried on by the Irregulars is without moral sanction: and therefore the killing of national soldiers in the course of it is murder before God; the seizing of public or private property is robbery; the breaking of roads, bridges, and railways, is criminal destruction; the invasion of homes and the molestation of citizens is a grievous crime. All those who, in contravention of this teaching, participate in such crimes, are guilty of the gravest sins, and may not be absolved in Confession, nor admitted to Holy Communion, if they propose to persevere in such evil courses. It is said that there are some priests who approve of this Irregular insurrection. If there be any such, they are false to their sacred office, and are guilty of the gravest scandal, and will not be allowed to retain the faculties they hold from us. Furthermore we, each for his own diocese, hereby forbid under pain of suspension, *ipso facto*, reserved to the ordinary, any priest to advocate or encourage this revolt, publicly or privately.

Our people will observe that in all this there is no question of mere politics, but of what is morally right or wrong according to the Divine Law, in certain principles, and in a certain series of acts, whether carried out for political purposes or otherwise. What we condemn is the armed campaign now being carried on against the government set up by the nation. If any section in the community have a grievance, or disapprove of the national government, they have the elections to fall back upon, and such constitutional action as is recognised by God and civilised society. If their political views are founded on wisdom they will succeed sooner or later; but, one thing is certain, the Hand of Providence will not be forced, nor their caused advanced, by irreligion and crime.

It may perhaps be said that in this our teaching we wound the strong feelings of many of our people. That we know, and the thought is an agony to us. But we must teach the Truth in this grave crisis, no matter what the consequences. It is not for want of sympathy with any part of our flock that we interfere, but from a deep and painful sense of our duty to God, to our people, and out of true charity to the young men themselves specially concerned. Let it not be said that this our teaching is due to political bias, and a desire to help one political party. If that were true, we were unworthy of our sacred office. Our religion, in such a supposition, were a mockery and a sham. We issue this Pastoral letter under the gravest sense of our responsibility, mindful of the charge laid upon us by our Divine Father, to preach His doctrine and safeguard His sacred rule of faith and morals, at any cost. We must, in the words of St Peter, 'Obey God rather than men'.

With all earnestness we appeal to the leaders of this saddest revolt to rise above their own feelings, to remember the claims of God, and the sufferings of the people, on their conscience; and to abandon methods which they now know, beyond the shadow of doubt, are un-Catholic and immoral, and look to the realisation of their ideals along lines sanctioned by Divine Law and the usages of well ordered society. Let them not think that we are insensible to their feelings. We think of them with compassion, carrying as they do on their shoulders the heavy responsibility for what is now happening in Ireland. Once more we beg and implore the young men of this movement, in the name of God, to return to their innocent homes, and make, if necessary, the big sacrifice of their own feelings for the common good. And surely it is no humiliation, having done their best, to abide by the verdict of Ireland.

We know that some of them are troubled and held back by the oath they took. A lawful oath is indeed a sacred bond between God and man; but no oath can bind any man to carry on a warfare against his own country, in circumstances forbidden by the law of God. It would be an offence to God and to the very nature of an oath to say so.

We, therefore, hope and pray that they will take advantage of the government's present offer, and make peace with their own country; a peace which will bring both happiness and honour to themselves, and joy to Ireland generally, and to the friends of Ireland all over the world.

In the lamentable upheaval, the moral sense of the people has, we fear, been badly shaken. We read with horror of the many murders recorded in the press. With feelings of shame we observe, that when country houses and public buildings were destroyed the furniture and other fittings were seized and carried away by people in the neighbourhood. We remind them that all such property belongs in justice to the original owners, and now must be preserved for and restored to them by those who hold it.

We desire to impress on the people the duty of supporting the national government, whatever it is; to set their faces resolutely against disorder; to pay their taxes, rents and annuities; and to assist the government, in every possible way, to restore order and establish peace. Unless they learn to do so, they can have no government; and, if they have no government, they can have no nation.

As human effort is fruitless without God's blessing, we exhort our priests and people to continue the prayers already ordered, and we direct that the remaining October devotions be offered up for peace. We also direct that a Novena to the Irish Saints, for the same end, be said in all public churches and oratories, and in semi-public oratories, to begin on the 28th of October and end on November the 5th, in preparation for the Feast of all the Irish Saints. These Novena devotions, in addition to the Rosary and Benediction, may include a special prayer for Ireland and the Litany of the Irish Saints.

APPENDIX 3

1931 Pastoral

Dearly beloved in Christ,

Assembled in Maynooth for our annual October meeting and deeply conscious of our responsibility for the Faith and Morals of our people, we cannot remain silent in face of the growing evidence of a campaign of Revolution and Communism, which if allowed to run its course unchecked must end in the ruin of Ireland, both soul and body.

You have no need to be told that there is in active operation amongst us a society of a militarist character whose avowed object is to overthrow the state by force of arms. In pursuit of this aim they arrogate to themselves the right to terrorise public officials and conscientious jury men, to intimidate decent citizens into silence or acquiescence, and even to take human life itself. Such methods and principles of action are in direct opposition to the law of God and come clearly under the definite condemnation of the Catholic Church; nor can the deeds of bloodshed to which they lead be made legitimate by any motive of patriotism.

To guard against misrepresentation, it is to be clearly understood that this statement which we feel called upon to issue has reference only to the religious and moral aspects of affairs and involves no judgment from us on any question of public policy so far as it is purely political. The political issue is a matter for the country at large and is to be decided by the votes of the people as a whole. But no policy, however good, may be prosecuted by methods and means like those we have referred to, which are contrary to Divine Law and subversive of social order.

The existing government in Saorstát Éireann is composed of our own countrymen and has been entrusted with office by the votes of the people. If the majority of the electors are not in agreement with its policy or its work they can set it aside by their votes and return to another to take its place. But so long as the government hold office it is the only lawful civil authority, a proposition that would be equally true if the government were defeated tomorrow and if any of the opposition parties assumed responsibility. From this it follows that no individuals or combination are free to resist its decrees or its officials by armed force, violence or intimidation. If such things were lawful, if any body of people who felt they were aggrieved were free to set up a rival executive and a rival army, the inevitable result must be anarchy, the destruction of personal liberty and the material as well as spiritual ruin of the country.

Side by side with the society referred to is a new organisation entitled 'Saor Éire' which is frankly *communistic* in its aims. The published programme, as reported in the press, when reduced to simple language is amongst other things to mobilise the workers and the working farmers of Ireland behind a revolutionary movement to set up a Communistic state. That is: to impose upon the Catholic soil of Ireland the same materialistic regime, with its fanatical hatred of God, as now dominates Russia and threatens to dominate Spain.

This organisation, which is but a translation into Irish life, under Bolshevistic tuition, of a similar scheme in use in Russia, proposes to attain its object by starting throughout the country districts wherever it can and in towns and amongst industrial workers what they call 'working peasant clubs' or 'cells' disguised for the moment in terms of nationality and zeal for farmers and workmen but which are to serve as revolutionary units to infect their disciples with the virus of Communism and create social disruption by organised opposition to the law of the land.

Thus are we to see, if their efforts are successful, the ruin of all that is dear to us in history, religion and country, brought about in the name of patriotism and humanity. For materialistic Communism in its principles and action wherever it appears. means a blasphemous denial of God and the overthrow of Christian civilisation. It means also class warfare, the abolition of private property and the destruction of family life.

In the words of our Holy Father:

Communism teaches and pursues a two-fold aim: merciless class warfare and complete abolition of private ownership. And this it does, not in secret and by hidden methods, but openly, frankly and by every means even the most violent. To obtain these ends Communists shrink from nothing and fear nothing; and when they have attained to power, it is unbelievable, indeed it seems portentous, how cruel and inhuman they show themselves to be. Evidence for this is the ghastly destruction and ruin with which they have laid waste immense tracts of Eastern Europe and

Asia, which their antagonism and open hostility to Holy Church and to God himself are, alas, only too well known and proved by their deeds.

We do not think it necessary to warn upright and faithful children of the Church against the impious and nefarious character of Communism. But we cannot contemplate without sorrow the heedlessness of those who seem to make light of these imminent dangers and with stolid indifference allow the propagation far and wide of those doctrines which seek by violence and bloodshed the destruction of all society. It is our duty to tell our people plainly that the two organisations to which we have referred, whether separate or in alliance, are sinful and irreligious and that no Catholic can lawfully be a member of them.

We appeal most earnestly and with deepest anxiety to all our people and especially the young, who through misguided counsels or mistaken love of country have been caught in the meshes of those evil associations, to abandon them at once at any price. Surely the ranks of the Communistic revolution are no place for an Irish boy of Catholic instincts. You cannot be a Catholic and a Communist. One stands for Christ, the other for anti-Christ. Neither can you, and for the same reason, be an ancillary of Communism.

Furthermore we appeal, and with all the earnestness we can command, to men of all political parties who love their religion and country to forget their differences for the time being and join their forces in an endeavour to find a solution for our social and economic problems that shall be in accordance with the traditions of Catholic Ireland.

With anxious hearts we turn to God who has mercifully watched over our country through the ages to extend his protecting arm to her now; to save her from horrors of civil strife and religious ruin; to open all eyes to the danger impending over us; and to strengthen all hearts to resist the forces of evil and unflinching faith.

We know, and it is a consolation to us, how sincerely Catholic our people are as a body; but in view of the peculiar enemies that are now assailing divine faith, our very feeling of security may become a source of danger.

As an act of expiation and to invoke the divine aid and the blessing of peace, we hereby direct that a triduum of prayer be opened in every parish church and in all religious houses on

Tuesday the 3rd of November in preparation for the Feast of all the Irish Saints, the devotions to consist of the Rosary and the Litany of the Irish Saints in presence of the blessed sacrament exposed. We call upon our people to join in these devotions with the utmost zeal and fervour.

The religious behind their convent walls will, we know, give Ireland in her hour of trial the benefit of their prayers. And we expect all our teachers to urge the children under their care, both boys and girls, to join in the same crusade of prayer.

Finally we direct our priests to exert every effort to keep young people from secret societies and diligently instruct them on the malice of murder and the satanic tendencies of Communism.

Praying for the mercy and blessing of God upon our country, we remain your faithful servants in Christ.

APPENDIX 4

May 1970 Statement of Northern Bishops

In recent weeks many people have expressed anxiety about increasing violence in Northern Ireland. People are worried about the course events may take during the coming election campaign and throughout the summer. In these circumstances we feel it our duty to give expression to certain thoughts and moral principles which we know are already in the minds and hearts of our people as a whole.

The overwhelming majority of our people do not want violence. They realise that it is morally wrong and that it is doubly so in Northern Ireland at the present time because of what it may lead to. It could lead to great suffering and death. It could lead to a repetition of the horrors we endured last autumn and even worse. And, as always, the people who would suffer most are the innocent and the poor. The people who are mourning their dead of last August, the people who had to spend last winter in wooden shacks, know what violence leads to. The Catholic people as a whole abhor it.

Since this is the case it would be a betrayal of the Catholic community — a stab in the back — for any individual, or group, to take it upon themselves to deliberately provoke violent incidents. So far as our people are concerned this would be quite a new turn of events but there is some evidence that it may have happened in recent days. If this is so then in the name of God and the whole Catholic community we condemn it.

Such evil initiatives are contrary to the law of Christ and must bring harm to thousands of innocent people. Moreover if such acts can be pointed to as the beginning of serious trouble it is not the handful of self-appointed activists who will be blamed but the whole Catholic community. Already people are not above suggesting that what has happened in recent days convicts the Catholic community for what happened last August.

It is no justification for such conduct to say that there was provocation or to say, even with some justice, that much worse deeds have been done by others and have gone unpunished. Two wrongs do not make a right.

Already the effects of recent incidents are being felt in the strain and illness and economic pressure which innocent people are suffering. No one has the right to inflict a situation of this kind on the people.

We therefore ask our people to make their voices heard in repudiation of individuals or groups who may appear to be interested in a continuation of violence. We ask them to co-operate with those groups who genuinely reflect the peaceful intentions of the people as a whole and who are working hard to restrain militant elements. We appeal in a particular way to the women — who are often the people who suffer most — and to parents. Your children could be maimed for life, physchologically and otherwise, by a continuation of these disturbances. There are many deep-seated wrongs to be undone in our society. Violence will only delay the day when they can be removed.

Significant changes have taken place with regard to the position of the minority in Northern Ireland during the past eighteen months. We regard it as essential that the programme of reform be adhered to, without any deviation, and pursued to its logical conclusion of fair treatment for all, in fact as well as in law. As these changes — and other vitally important changes which have been promised — take effect there will be a genuine prospect of justice and peace and further progress by orderly means. To anyone who thinks rationally about the future of the people concerned — and it is the people, human beings, that matter, not causes or ideologies — there can be no question of where the choice must lie between the violent way and the peaceful way. We warn those few individuals who would opt for the violent way that they have absolutely no mandate from the people.

The principles of our Christian faith, which must be our supreme guide, powerfully reinforce the message of reason and common sense. Next to the love of God the greatest commandment is love our neighbour. One neighbour, as the catechism teaches us, is 'mankind of every description, even those who injure us or differ from us in religion.' Most of our neighbours here are our fellow-Christians, united with us in the love and worship of the same God and the same Lord and Saviour Jesus Christ.

There may be moments when this most difficult of all commandments calls for almost superhuman restraint. Even then we are bound by it. If we have recourse to God in prayer he will not deny us the grace to be faithful to this His great commandment.

This May 1970 statement did not deal with the reasons for the civil rights protests and the violent reaction of the Unionists. It ignored the violence inflicted on the peaceful PD marches at Burntollet in January 1970 of that year. It ignored the brutality of the RUC and the B men who murdered a man, Samuel Devenny, in his own house in the Bogside in 1969. The bishops had not been present at the protests to see the bigotry and brutality in Dungannon, Derry, Lurgan and Newry. In spite of the clear teaching of the Second Vatican Council this statement failed to address the basic injustice. It was as if the Second Vatican Council had never happened. It was as if nothing was happening in the Church any where else in the world. It might well have been written in 1916, 1857 or 1798.

In spite of the 50 years of corrupt Unionist rule since Ireland was forcibly partitioned the bishops did not question that status quo. There had been pogroms and sectarian murder of Catholics, systematic discrimination, repressive laws, special police, denial of human and civil rights, and every possible kind of humiliation but the Catholic hierarchy had no words of protest.

STATEMENT
9 November 1987

The Standing Committee of the Irish Bishops issued the following statement from their meeting today and they ask that it be read at all Masses next Sunday:

1. After nearly twenty years of violence in the north the language of condemnation has become worn and emotions have been dulled by too long exposure to atrocity and tragedy. Yet recent events have evoked among our people a new sense of revulsion and shame at the depth to which our country is being dragged.

2. People have been appalled by the elemental savagery surrounding the kidnapping of Mr John O'Grady and his barbaric treatment in captivity.

3. It is long since there has been such a sense of disgust throughout the Catholic community as Sunday's explosion in Enniskillen has aroused.

4. There is in the Catholic community north and south a strong desire to find some way of collectively expressing our sympathy and solidarity with the Protestant community in this tragedy. During these days we ask people to come to week-day Masses in large numbers so that the whole population may be united in repentance, sorrow and prayer at this terrible time. Everything should be done to demonstrate Catholic revulsion at these crimes and to dissociate the Catholic community completely from those who carry out such deeds.

5. There is no room for ambivalence. In face of the present campaigns of republican violence the choice of all Catholics is clear. It is a choice between good and evil.

6. It is sinful to join organisations committed to violence or to remain in them. It is sinful to support such organisations or to call on others to support them.

7. We sympathise with the police forces north and south in their task of upholding the law in most difficult and dangerous circumstances. Many of their members have lost their lives. Many others, like Garda O'Connor, have suffered serious injury in this task. We call on all our people to co-operate with the police in bringing the guilty to justice.

8. It has become clear that dotted across this country there are safe houses provided for members of these organisations. There are people who store weapons or who willingly help fugitives to escape. We say very solemnly to these people that they share in the awful crime of murder. People must choose. There is no longer any room for romantic illusion. There is no excuse for thinking that the present violence in Ireland can be morally justified.

9. In face of these recent crimes let us redouble our prayers that the Lord will remove the veil from the eyes of those who will not see and bring about in our hearts a true spirit of repentance.

10 May Mary Queen of Peace pray for us all to her Son that he may grant us his gift of peace.

Notes

Full references for authors and titles of works are given in the Bibliography.

INTRODUCTION
1. *Lucha Struggle — A Journal of Christian Reflection on Struggles for Liberation,* New York, September/October, 1988. 2. *Ibid.* 3. *Renewing the Earth,* ed by David O'Brien and Thomas A. Shannon, Image Books, New York, 1977. 4. *The Way Forward?* Des Wilson and Oliver Kearney, Springhill Community House, Belfast, 1988.

CHAPTER 1
1. Frank Gallagher, *The Indivisible Island,* Victor Gollancz, London, 1957, p. 33. 2. Kevin Whelan in an unpublished article 'The Regional Impact of Irish Catholicism 1700-1850'. 3. *Clogher Record,* 1954. Material translated by P J Flanagan. 4. Dorothy Macardle *The Irish Republic,* Irish Press, Dublin, 1951, p. 36. 5. James Connolly, *Labour in Irish History,* New Books, 1983, p. 13. 6. S J Connolly, *Priests and People in Pre-Famine Ireland 1780-1845,* Dublin, Gill & Macmillan, 1982, p. 10. 7. Matthias Buschkuhl, *Great Britain and the Holy See 1746-1870,* Dublin, Irish Academic Press, 1982, p. 24. 8. *History and Antiquities of the Diocese of Ossory,* by Rev. W Carrigan, Dublin, 1905, p. 186ff. 9. Buschkuhl, p. 25. 10. *Ibid,* p. 25. 11. *Ibid.,* p. 29. 12. *Ibid.,* p. 25. 13. John Healy, *Maynooth College 1795-1895,* Browne and Nolan, Dublin, 1895, p. 98. 14. *Ibid.,* p. 99. 15. Buschkuhl, p. 33. 16. Buschkuhl, p. 38. 17. *Ibid.,* p. 38. 18. Kevin Whelan, article in *Wexford History and Society,* Geography Publications, Dublin, 1987, p. 296. 19. *Ibid.,* p. 297. 20. *Ibid.,* p. 298. 21. *Ibid.,* p. 298. 22. *Ibid.,* p. 298. 23. *Ibid.,* p. 299. 24. *Ibid.,* p. 299-300. 25. *Ibid.,* p. 301-302. 26. Healy, p. 118-119. 27. *Ibid.,* p. 119. 28. *Ibid.,* p. 241. 29. *Ibid.,* p. 244 30. *Ibid.,* p. 244. 31. *Ibid.,* p. 244. 32. *Ibid.,* p. 244. 33. *Ibid.,* p. 244. 34. *Ibid.,* p. 245. 35. *Ibid.,* p. 245. 36. *Ibid.,* p. 245.

CHAPTER 2

1. Healy, p. 119. 2. Buschkuhl, p. 43. 3. Donal A. Kerr, *Peel, Priests and Politics*, Claredon Press, Oxford 1982, p. 241. 4. Healy, p. 240. 5. Oliver MacDonagh, *States of Mind*, George Allen and Unwin, London, 1983, p. 94. 6. Buschkuhl, p. 76. 7. MacDonagh, p. 95. 8. Buschkuhl, p. 78. 9. *Ibid.*, p. 78. 10. MacDonagh, p. 96. 11. Buschkuhl, p. 84. 12. Buschkuhl, p. 85. 13. Buschkuhl, p. 84. 14. Buschkuhl, p. 85. 15. Buschkuhl, p. 84. 16. Buschkuhl, p. 84. 17. Buschkuhl, p. 85. 18. Emmet Larkin, *The Consolidation of the Irish Church 1869-1870*, p. 20. 19. *Eire — Ireland*, Fomhar, 1987. Article by Patricia Twomey Ryan. 20. *Ibid.* 21. Buschkuhl, p. 211. 22. *Monthly Review*, (An Independent Socialist Magazine), New York, January, 1986. Article by John Newsinger, p. 16. 23. *Ibid.*, p. 17. 24. *Ibid.*, p. 17. 25. *Ibid.*, p. 18. 26. *Ibid.*, p. 18. 27. *Bishop Duggan; The Patriot Prelate* — Pamphlet.

CHAPTER 3

1. *Monthly Review*, Article by John Newsinger, p. 19. 2. *Ibid.*, p. 19. 3. *Ibid.*, p. 19. 4. *Ibid.*, p. 21. 5. *Freeman's Journal*, 11 April, 1916. 6. On 5 October, 1915, *The Irish News* carried a report on a British army recruiting rally in Derry to which the Catholic Bishop, Most Rev Dr McHugh wrote apologising for his inability to attend and adding that he was 'in complete sympathy with the object of your meeting and I take advantage of this opportunity to express my earnest wish that the response to your appeal may be in keeping with the requirements of the crisis through which we are passing.' 7. *Eirí Amach na Cásca*, Republican Publications, Dublin, 1986. Article by Nollaig Ó Gadhra, p. 68ff. 8. *Ibid.*, p. 72. 9. *Ibid.*, p. 72. 10. *Ibid.*, p. 72. 11. *Ibid.*, p. 72. 12. *Ibid.*, p. 72. 13. *Guerrilla Days in Ireland*, Tom Barry, The Irish Press, 1949, Anvil Books, 1981, p. 56. 14. *Capuchin Annual*, 1970. Article by Tomas Ó Fiaich 'The Catholic Clergy and the Independence Movement', p. 480ff. 15. Michael Farrell, *Northern Ireland: The Orange State*, Pluto Press, London, 1976, p. 67. 16. Frances Blake, *The Irish Civil War*, Information on Ireland, London 1986, p. 43. 17. Farrell, p. 62. 18. Michael Ó Riordain, *Connolly Column*, New Books, Dublin, 1979, p. 198. 19. Blake, p. 45. 20. Blake, p. 53. 21. 'A Protestant parliament and a Protestant state'— the description of the state given by Craigavon in April 1934, see Farrell, p. 92. 22. Farrell, p. 101. 23. Farrell, p. 101. 24. Farrell, p. 102. 25. Farrell, p. 103. 26. Farrell, p.134 27. Ó Riordain, p. 202.

28. J H Whyte, *Church and State in Modern Ireland 1923-1979,* Gill and Macmillan, Dublin, 1971, p. 320. **29.** Michel Peillon, *Contemporary Irish Society,* Gill and Macmillan, Dublin, 1982, p. 89.

CHAPTER 4

1. Denis Carroll, *What is Liberation Theology?* Mercier Press, Cork & Dublin 1987, p. 19-20. **2.** *Concilium* — an international journal of theology. Issue on 'Option for the Poor'; Article by Rainer Kampling, p. 51ff. **3.** Herman Dorries, *Constantine the Great,* Harper Torchbooks, New York, 1972, p. 134. **4.** Charles Avila, *Ownership: Early Christian Teaching,* Orbis, Maryknoll/Sheed and Ward, London 1983, p. 35. **5.** *Ibid.,* p. 132. **6.** *Ibid.,* p. 132., **7.** *Ibid.,* p. 133., **8.** *Ibid.,* p. 135. **9.** *Concilium,* Article by Rainer Kampling, p. 51ff. **10.** Alan Schreck, *The Compact History of the Catholic Church,* Servant Books, Ann Arbor, Michigan, 1987, p. 36. **11.** *Monthly Review,* July/August, 1984, Article by Dorothee Sollee. **12.** Jose Miguez Bonino, *Doing Theology in a Revolutionary Situation,* Fortress Press, Philadelphia, 1975, p. 8. **13.** *Ibid.,* p. 19. **14.** *Ibid.,* p. 19. **15.** Walbert Buhlmann, *The Coming of the Third Church,* St Paul Publications, Slough, 1976, p. 27. **16.** Helder Camara, *The Church and Colonialism,* Dimension Books, Denville, New Jersey, 1969. **17.** Penny Lernoux, *Cry of the People,* Penguin Books, 1982, pp. 3-81.

CHAPTER 5

1. *National Catholic Reporter,* 31 October, 1986. **2.** Donal Dorr, *Option for the Poor,* Gill and Macmillan/Orbis, Dublin and New York, 1983. **3.** *Ibid.* **4.** *Ibid.* **5.** Camara, p. 109. **6.** J Philip Wogaman, *Christian Perspectives on Politics,* SCM Press Ltd, London, 1988. **7.** *Challenge to the Church — The Kairos Document,* Catholic Institute for International Relations, London, 1985, p. 11. **8.** *Ibid.,* p.12. **9.** *Ibid.,* p. 12. **10.** *Ibid.,* p. 13. **11.** *Ibid.,* p. 14. **12.** Alvaro Barreiro, *Basic Ecclesial Communities,* Orbis, Maryknoll, New York, 1982. **13.** *St Anthony Messenger,* November, 1982. Article by Penny Lernoux, 'The Changing Church in Latin America'. **14.** Essays by Jon Sobrino and Ignacio Martin Baro, *Archbishop Oscar Romero — Voice of the Voiceless,* Orbis, Maryknoll, New York, 1985. **15.** Barreiro. **16.** *St Anthony Messenger,* November, 1982, article by Penny Lernoux. **17.** *Ibid.* **18.** *Instruction on Certain Aspects of the Theology of Liberation,* CTS, London, 1984. **19.** *Instruction on Christian Freedom and Liberation,* CTS, London, 1986. **20.** *Lucha Struggle,* Jan/Feb 1988. **21.** *Ibid.* **22.** *Ibid.* **23.** *Ibid.*

CHAPTER 6

1. *Challenge to the Church — The Kairos Document;* Sobrino and Baro and also Thomas D Hanks, *God So Loved the Third World*, Orbis, Maryknoll, New York, p. 105ff. **2.** *Principles of Catholic Theology,* edited by Edward J Gratsch, Alba House, New York, 1981, p. 318ff. **3.** Jon P Gunnermann, *The Moral Meaning of Revolution,* Yale University Press, New Haven and London, 1979. **4.** Pope Paul VI's encyclical, *Populorum Progressio.* **5.** *Instruction on Christian Freedom and Liberation.* **6.** Carroll, pp. 75ff. **7.** *Speeches of Pope John Paul II in Ireland*, Veritas, Dublin, 1980. **8.** *The Gospel and Struggle,* Louie Hechanova, CIIR, London, 1986, pp. 18ff. **9.** *Challenge to the Church — The Kairos Document.*

CHAPTER 7

1. *A Life of Poverty — N. Ireland*, published by the Northern Ireland Poverty Lobby and the Social Policy Society, Jordanstown, 1986. **2.** *Ibid.*, p. 23. **3.** *Ibid.*, p. 18. **4.** *Ibid.*, p. 18. **5.** *The People's Bulletin,* November/December 1987. **6.** *Ibid.* **7.** Maurice Burke, *Britain's War Machine in Ireland*, Oisin Publications, New York City, 1987.

CHAPTER 8

1. *Justice, Love and Peace (Pastoral Letters of the Irish Bishops, 1969-1979)*, Veritas, Dublin, 1979. p. 38. **2.** *Ibid.* **3.** CONCERNED published by Fermanagh Resistance Committee, 22 January, 1972. **4.** *Social Studies* — Irish Journal of Sociology, February/March 1973. Article by C B Daly. **5.** *Ibid.* **6.** *Ibid.* **7.** Quoted by British Information Services Washington, November, 1982. **8.** Bishop C B Daly's Sermon in Twinbrook on 24 April 1988 published by Shanway Press under the title *Time for a New Deal.* **9.** *Justice, Love and Peace,* p.39. **10.** *Ibid.*, p. 40. **11.** C B Daly, *Peace — the Work of Justice, Addresses on the Northern Tragedy (1973-79)*, Veritas, Dublin, 1979. **12.** *Violence — A Report to the Churches*, Christian Journals Ltd, Belfast, 1979. **13.** Wilson and Kearney.

CHAPTER 9

1. Donal Dorr's translation of opening lines of the Second Vatican Council's document *Gaudium et Spes.* **2.** *Challenge to the Church — The Kairos Document.* **3.** O'Brien and Shannon. **4.** *Pope John Paul II — Speeches in Ireland.* **5.** *Challenge to the Church.*

Bibliography

CATHOLIC CHURCH HISTORY

Buschkuhl, Matthias, *Great Britain and the Holy See 1746-1870*, Irish Academic Press Ltd, Dublin, 1982.

Gonzalez, Justo L., *The Story of Christianity: Vol I: The Early Church to the Dawn of the Reformation*, Harper & Row, Publishers Inc., New York, 1984.

Healy, John, *Maynooth College: Its Centenary History*, Browne & Nolan, Dublin, 1895.

MacCulloch, Diarmaid, *Groundwork of Christian History*, Epworth Press, Westminster, London, 1987.

Orlandis, Jose, *A Short History of the Catholic Church*, Four Courts Press Ltd, Dublin, 1983.

Schreck, Alan, *The Compact History of the Catholic Church*, Servant Books, Ann Arbor, Michigan, 1987.

CATHOLIC THEOLOGY

Byrne, Tony, C S Sp, *Working for Justice & Peace — A Practical Guide*, Mission Press, Ndola, Zambia, 1988.

Gratsch, Edward J. *et al*, (1981) *Principles of Catholic Theology* (A Synthesis of Dogma and Morals), Society of St Paul, Alba House New York, 1981.

O'Brien, David J & Shannon, Thomas A (ed.) *Renewing the Earth* (Catholic Documents on Peace, Justice and Liberation), Image Books, New York, 1977.

Rahner, Karl, *Encyclopedia of Theology* (A concise Sacramentum Mundi), Burns & Oates Ltd., London, 1975.

Veritas Publications, *Justice, Love & Peace*, (Pastoral Letters of the Irish Bishops 1969-79), Veritas Publications, Dublin, 1979.

Walsh, Michael & Davies Brian (ed.), *Proclaiming Justice and Peace* (Documents from John XXIII to John Paul II), Collins Liturgical Publications, London, 1984.

Wogaman, J. Philip, *Christian Perspectives on Politics*, S C M Press Ltd, London, 1988.

LIBERATION THEOLOGY

Avila, Charles, *Ownership: Early Christian Teaching*, Orbis Books, Maryknoll, New York and Sheed & Ward Ltd., London 1983.

Assmann, Hugo, *Theology for a Nomad Church*, Search Press Ltd, London, 1975.

Barreiro, Alvaro, *Basic Ecclesial Communities*, Orbis Books, Maryknoll, New York, 1982.

Berryman, Phillip, *Liberation Theology*, I B Tauris & Co. Ltd, London, 1978.

Bigo, Pierre, SJ, *The Church and Third World Revolution*, Orbis Boods, Maryknoll, New York, 1977.

Boff, Leonardo, *Way of the Cross — Way of Justice*, Orbis Books, Maryknoll, New York, 1980.

Boff, Leonardo and Clodovis, *Introducing Liberation Theology*, Burnes & Oates/Search Press Ltd, London, 1987.

Bonino, Jose Miguez, *Doing Theology in a Revolutionary Situation*, Fortress Press, Philadelphia, 1975.

Buhlmann, Walbert, *The Coming of the Third Church*, St Paul Publications, Slough, 1976.

Cardenal, Ernesto, *The Gospel in Solentiname, Vol.I*, Orbis Books, Maryknoll, New York, 1976.

Carroll, Denis, *What is Liberation Theology?*, Mercier Press Ltd, Cork/Fowler Wright Books Ltd, England 1987.

Camara, Dom Helder, *The Church and Colonialism — The Betrayal of the Third World*, Dimension Books Ltd, Denville, New Jersey, 1969.

Clery, Edward L, OP, *Crisis and Change — The Church in Latin America Today*, Orbis Books, Maryknoll, New York, 1985.

Comblin, Jose, *Sent from the Father — Meditations on the Fourth Gospel*, Gill and Macmillan Ltd, Dublin, 1979.

Comblin, Jose, *Cry of the Oppressed, Cry of Jesus* (Meditations on Scripture and Contemporary Struggle), Orbis Books, Maryknoll, New York, 1988.

Cone, James H, *Speaking the Truth — Ecumenism, Liberation and Black Theology*, Wm B Eerdmans Publishing Co, Grand Rapids, Michigan, 1986.

Cort, John C, *Christian Socialism — An Informal History*, Orbis Books, Maryknoll, New York, 1988.

de la Torre, Edicio, *Touching Ground, Taking Root*, (Theological and Political Reflections on the Philippine Struggle), The Catholic

Institute for International Relations London/in association with the British Council of Churches, London, 1986.

Drummond, Richard Henry, *Toward a New Age in Christian Theology*, Orbis Books, Maryknoll, New York, 1985.

Dussell, Enrique, *Philosophy of Liberation*, Orbis Books, Maryknoll, New York, 1985.

Galilea, Segundo, *Following Jesus*, Orbis Books, Maryknoll, New York, 1981.

Haight, Roger, SJ, *An Alternative Vision*, (An Interpretation of Liberation Theology), Paulist Press, New York, 1985.

Hechanova, Louie, *The Gospel and Struggle*, CIIR, London 1986.

Jerez, Cesar, SJ, *The Church and the Nicaraguan Revolution*, (CIIR Justice Papers no. 5), Catholic Institute for International Relations, London, 1984.

Jesudasan, Ignatius SJ, *A Gandhian Theology of Liberation*, Orbis Books, Maryknoll, New York, 1984.

Lernoux, Penny, *Cry of the People* (The Struggle for Human Rights in Latin America), Penguin Books, 1980, 1982.

Mesters, Carlos, O Carm., *The Road to Freedom*, Veritas Publications, Dublin, 1974.

Pallares, Jose Cardenas, *A Poor Man Called Jesus*, (Reflections on the Gospel of Mark), Orbis Books, Maryknoll, New York, 1986.

Paoli, Arturo, *Gather Together in My Name* (Reflections on Christianity and Community), Orbis Books, Maryknoll, New York, 1987.

Pico, Juan Hernandez, SJ, /Sobrino Jon, SJ, *Theology of Christian Solidarity*, Orbis Books, Maryknoll, New York, 1985.

Planas, Ricardo, *Liberation Theology — The Political Expression of Religion*, Sheed & Ward, Kansas City, 1986.

Reding, Andrew (ed.) *Christianity and Revolution*, (Tomas Borge's Theology of Life), Orbis Books, Maryknoll, New York, 1987.

Regan, David, CSSp, *Church Liberation — A Pastoral Portrait of the Church in Brazil*, Dominican Publications Ltd, Dublin/Fowler Wright Books Ltd, England, 1987.

Shaull, Richard, *Heralds of a New Reformation — The Poor of South and North America*, Orbis Books, Maryknoll, New York, 1984.

Sobrino, Jon, *Jesus in Latin America*, Orbis Books, Maryknoll, New York, 1987.

Tamez, Elsa, *Bible of the Oppressed*, Orbis Books, Maryknoll, New York, 1982.

Torres, Sergio/Eagleson, John (ed.), *The Challenge of Basic Christian Communities*, Orbis Books, Maryknoll, New York, 1981.

Wilson, Des, *An End to Silence*, The Mercier Press, Cork & Dublin, 1985. Royal Carbery Books, Cork, 1987.

CHURCH AND STATE   (in Ireland and Elsewhere)

Burke, W P, *Irish Priests in the Penal Times (1660-1760)*, Irish University Press, Shannon, 1968.

Connolly, Seán, *Religion and Society in Nineteenth Century Ireland* (Studies in Irish Economic and Social History 3), The Economic and Social History Society of Ireland, UCD, 1985.

Connolly, SJ, *Priests and People in Pre-Famine Ireland — 1780-1845*, Gill and Macmillan Ltd, Dublin 1982.

Corish, Patrick, *The Irish Catholic Experience — a Historical Survey*, Gill and Macmillan Ltd, Dublin, 1985.

Dorries, Hermann, *Constantine The Great*, Harper and Row Publishers, New York, 1972.

Hughes, Philip, *A Popular History of the Catholic Church*, Burnes and Oates, London, 1985.

Inglis, Tom, *Moral Monopoly: The Catholic Church in Modern Irish Society*, Gill and Macmillan Ltd, Dublin, 1987.

Keenan, Desmond, *The Catholic Church in Nineteenth Century Ireland*, Gill and Macmillan, 1983.

O'Shea, James, *Priest, Politics and Society in Post-famine Ireland*, Wolfhound Press:Dublin/Humanities Press:New Jersey, 1983.

Siegel, Paul N, *The Meek and the Militant — Religion and Power Across the World*, Zed Books Ltd, London and New Jersey, 1986.

Whyte, J H, *Church & State in Modern Ireland 1923-1979*, Second Edition, Gill and Macmillan Ltd, Dublin, 1971, 1980.

Veritas Publications, *Bishop of the Land War* (Dr Patrick Duggan, Bishop of Clonfert 1813-1896), Veritas Publications, Dublin, 1987.

IRISH HISTORY

Berresford, Ellis, P, *James Connolly — Selected Writings*, Monthly Review Press, New York and London, 1973.

Berresford, Ellis, P, *A History of the Irish Working Class*, Pluto Press, London and Sydney, 1972-1985.

Blake, Frances M, *The Irish Civil War and what it still means for the Irish People,* Information on Ireland, London, 1986.

Bowen, Desmond, *Paul Cardinal Cullen and the Shaping of Modern Irish Catholicism,* Gill and Macmillan, Dublin, 1983.

Boyd, Andrew, *Holy War in Belfast,* Anvil Books, 1969, Pretani Press, Belfast, 1988.

Boyd, Andrew, *Northern Ireland: Who is to Blame?,* The Mercier Press, Cork & Dublin, 1984.

Brown, Terence, *Ireland: a Social and Cultural History 1922-1979,* Fontana Paperbacks, Douglas, 1981.

Connolly, James (with introduction Allen, Kieran), *Labour in Irish History,* Bookmarks, London, Chicago and Melbourne, 1987.

Cronin, Seán, *The Revolutionaries,* Republican Publications, Dublin, 1971.

Cronin, Seán, *Irish Nationalism: A History of its Roots and Ideology,* Academy Press, Dublin, 1980.

Curtis Edmund, *A History of Ireland,* Methuen & Co. Ltd, New York, 1936, 1986.

de Paor, Liam, *The Peoples of Ireland,* Hutchinson and Co., London, 1986.

Farrell, Michael, *Northern Ireland: The Orange State,* Pluto Press Ltd, London, 1976, 1980.

Griffith, Kenneth & O'Grady, Timothy E, *Curious Journey (An Oral History of Ireland's Unfinished Revolution),* Hutchinson, London, 1982.

Heron, James Connolly, (ed.), *The Words of James Connolly,* The Mercier Press, Cork & Dublin, 1986.

Jackson, T A, (ed. C Desmond Greaves), *Ireland Her Own,* Lawrence and Wishart, London, 1976.

Kerr, Donal A, *Peel, Priests and Politics,* Clarendon Press, Oxford, 1982.

Lee, Joseph, *The Modernisation of Irish Society 1848-1918,* Gill and Macmillan, Dublin, 1973.

Macardle, Dorothy, *The Irish Republic,* Victor Gollancz Ltd, London and Irish Press Ltd, Dublin, 1937, 1957.

MacCall, Seamus, *A Little History of Ireland,* Dolmen Press Ltd, Portlaoise, 1973, 1986.

MacDonagh, Oliver, *States of Mind (A Study of Anglo-Irish Conflict 1780-1980),* George Allen & Unwin, London, Boston and Sydney, 1983.

O'Brien, Jack, *British Brutality in Ireland*, The Mercier Press, Cork & Dublin, 1989.

O'Leary, Peter, (trans C Ó Ceirín) *My Story — Reminiscences of a Life in Ireland from The Great Hunger to The Gaelic League*, Oxford University Press, Oxford and New York, 1987.

Ó Riordain, Micheal, *Connolly Column*, (The Story of the Irishmen who fought for the Spanish Republic 1936-1939), New Book Publications, Dublin, 1979.

Ó Snodaigh, Padraig & Mitchell, Arthur (ed.), *Irish Political Documents 1916-1949*, Irish Academic Press Ltd, Dublin, 1985.

Republican Publications (ed. MacGlynn, Pat), (1986) *Eirí Amach na Cásca — The Easter Rising 1916*, Republican Publications, Belfast and Dublin, 1986.

Wallace, Martin, *A Short History of Ireland*, David & Charles Publishers Ltd, London, 1973.

Whelan, Kevin (ed.), *Wexford History and Society*, (Interdisciplinary Essays on the History of an Irish County), Geography Publications, Dublin, 1987.

VIOLENCE AND NON-VIOLENCE

Fanon, Frantz, *The Wretched of the Earth*, Penguin, Middlesex, 1963.

Kitson, Frank, *Low Intensity Operations*, Faber, 1972.

Malcolm X (ed. George Breitman), *By Any Means Necessary*, Pathfinder, New York, 1970.

Merton, Thomas, *Gandhi on Non-Violence*, New Directions, New York, 1964.

MacBride, Seán, *A Message to the Irish People*, Mercier Press, Cork & Dublin, 1985.

Soelle, Dorothee, *Beyond Mere Obedience*, The Pilgrim Press, New York, 1982.

Tutu, Desmond, *Hope and Suffering*, Collins, Fount Paperbacks, London, 1983.

Tutu, Desmond, *Crying in the Wilderness*, William B Eerdmans Publishing Co, Grand Rapids, Michigan, 1982.

CONTEMPORARY STUDIES AND
REFLECTIONS ON THE IRISH STRUGGLE

Adams, Gerry, *The Politics of Irish Freedom*, Brandon, Dingle, 1986.

Adams, Gerry, *A Pathway to Peace*, The Mercier Press, Cork & Dublin, 1989.

A Life of Poverty: Northern Ireland, Published by The Social Policy Society, University of Ulster and N.I. Poverty Lobby, 1986.

Bambery, Chris, *Ireland's Permanent Revolution*, Bookmarks, London and Chicago, 1986.

Bell, Geoffrey, *The British in Ireland — a suitable case for withdrawal*, Pluto Press, London, 1984.

Benn, Tony, (ed. Chris Mullin) *Arguments for Socialism*, Penguin, Middlesex, 1979-80.

Burke, Maurice, *Britain's War Machine in Ireland*, Oisin Publications, New York, 1987.

Collins, Martin (ed.), *Ireland after Britain*, Pluto Press in association with Labour and Ireland, London, 1985.

Coughlan, Anthony, *Fooled Again?* The Mercier Press, Cork & Dublin, 1986.

Crotty, Raymond, *Ireland In Crisis*, Brandon, Dingle, 1986.

Curtis, Liz, *Ireland: The Propaganda War*, Pluto Press, London and Sydney, 1984.

Daly, Cahal B, *Peace — The Work of Justice* (Addresses on The Northern Tragedy 1973-79), Veritas, Dublin, 1979.

Doherty, Frank, *The Stalker Affair*, Mercier Press, Cork & Dublin, 1986.

Farrell, Michael, *Sheltering the Fugitive?* The Mercier Press, Cork & Dublin, 1985.

Feehan, John M, *Bobby Sands and the Tragedy of Northern Ireland*, The Mercier Press, Cork & Dublin, 1983.

Irish Republican Prisoners of War, Questions of History, Education Department, Sin Féin, 1987.

Kelley, Kevin, *The Longest War*, Brandon, Dingle, 1982.

Nothing But the Same Old Story — the roots of anti-Irish racism (1984) Published by Information on Ireland, London, 1984.

Ó hEithir, Breandán, *This is Ireland*, O'Brien Press, Dublin, 1987.

Ó hEithir, Breandán, *The Begrudgers Guide to Irish Politics*, Poolbeg, Dublin, 1986.

Peillon, Michel, *Contemporary Irish Society, an introduction*, Gill and Macmillan, Dublin, 1982.

Reed, David, *Ireland: The Key to the British Revolution*, Larkin Publications, London, 1984.

Sands, Bobby, *One Day In My Life*, The Mercier Press, Cork & Dublin, 1983.

Sands, Bobby, *Skylark Sing Your Lonely Song*, The Mercier Press, Cork & Dublin, 1985.

Shoot to Kill? International Lawyers Inquiry into the lethal use of Firearms by the Secutiry Forces in Northern Ireland, The Mercier Press, Cork & Dublin, 1985.

They Shoot Children, Information on Ireland, London, 1982, 1988.

Torture in the Eighties, Amnesty International Report, Martin Robertson and Amnesty International, London, 1984.

Violence in Ireland — a Report to the Churches, Christian Journals, Belfast.

Wilson, Des and Kearney, Oliver, *The Way Forward?* Springhill Community House, Belfast, 1988.